RUGBY
CHARACTERS

CARICATURES BY JOHN IRELAND

TEXT BY CLIFF MORGAN

STANLEY PAUL

LONDON · SYDNEY · AUCKLAND · JOHANNESBURG

Stanley Paul & Co Ltd

An imprint of Random Century
Random Century House
20 Vauxhall Bridge Road
London SW1V 2SA
Random Century Australia (Pty) Ltd
20 Alfred Street, Milsons Point, Sydney 2061, N.S.W.
Random Century New Zealand Ltd
191 Archers Road, PO Box 40–086, Glenfield, Auckland 10
Century Hutchinson South Africa (Pty) Ltd
PO Box 337, Bergvlei 2012, South Africa

First published 1990
© Lennard Books Ltd 1990

British Library Cataloguing in Publication Data

Ireland, John
Rugby Characters,
1 Rugby Football. Biographies.
Collections.
I. Title. II. Morgan, Cliff
796. 3330922

ISBN 0 09 174584 5

Made by Lennard Associates Ltd
Mackerye End, Harpenden, Hertfordshire AL5 5DR

Editor Michael Leitch
Design by Pocknell & Co
Typesetting by Jigsaw Graphics, Romford
Origination by Scantrans Pte Ltd, Singapore
Production Reynolds Clark Associates Ltd
Printed and bound in Yugoslavia by
Mladinska Knjiga, Ljubljana

CONTENTS

INTRODUCTION

WHEN I SAW THE caricature that John Ireland had produced of me for this book, my mind flashed back some 36 years to an evening when a cartoon of C.I. Morgan appeared in the late edition of the South Wales Echo. My mother's immediate reaction was typical of any mother, 'Well, I don't know about that. All I can say is that you were not born ugly, you must have been hit ugly in that old game you try to play'. No one like a mother to get down to the basics! What she did not appreciate at the time was that any caricature is simply a representation of an individual, which exaggerates the characteristic traits for comic effect. Over the years she actually grew to like the thing and she had it framed. It is one of the very few souvenirs I have of happy days playing the game. As I have aged and mellowed it also makes me smile and I would like to think that the rugby players included in this particular book will enjoy the work of John Ireland.

Selecting only forty is a daunting task and there are so many other fine figures that I would have liked to have seen on the following pages. It is impossible to do justice to a game and the people who make it such a pleasure. My apologies to those I care for who are not in the forty and to those who are, forgive my impertinence in assuming so much.

Rugby characters ... a prop forward called Cliff Davies who played for Cardiff, Wales, the Barbarians and the 1950 Lions is the one who left the greatest impression on me. He was a coal miner, singer, poet, part-time undertaker – but more importantly he was the finest of human beings, and the best of forwards with wit and wisdom and stubborn good sense. He was not capable of hurting or lying. There was a young Baptist minister ordained in the village on a Thursday night, he played second-row forward for the locals on the Saturday and everyone in the team went to hear him preach his first sermon on the following Sunday morning. Coming out of the Chapel, Cliff was asked what he thought of the new preacher. Like a flash he replied, 'Powerful in prayer but hopeless in the line-out.' Since Cliff Davies I have always tried to find something special in everyone I have been privileged to meet in a game that has given so much to so many young people for such a long time now; for everyone is, as the dictionary says about character, a combination of traits and qualities distinguishing the individual nature of a person.

THE FULL-BACKS

ON THE VILLAGE GREEN in South Clifton, Nottinghamshire stands a tree. It was planted by the folk there to honour the name of William Henry Hare, MBE – Freeman of the town of Newark. It is an oak, an appropriate species for 'Dusty' Hare who represents all that is stout, upright and strong, honourable and enduring in the game of rugby union which he has graced with such style and dignity. He inflicted pain on many a rugby team with his boot – scoring a record 7,191 points during a first-class career that sparkled for 20 years. Hare has won more matches with goal kicks than any other player, anywhere. The 240 points he scored for England in International matches is a record, as is the total of 44 points in the Five Nations Championship in the 1983-84 season.

But a computer could never calculate his real value. Cold statistics will never represent the qualities of the man or spell out the warm influence he discharged or the stability he gave to the players around him. He attracted loyalty and admiration, for he had the ability to engage totally his fellow human beings.

For 13 years he wore the jersey of Leicester with enormous pride and, with the exception of his first match for the club, he averaged ten points per match. Even the closest scrutiny of world rugby records will confirm that Dusty Hare has never had an equal as a goal-kicker. No argument, he was the greatest.

Like so many gifted sportsmen he could suffer lapses in concentration on the field. There were times when his daring made you close your eyes in disbelief as he tried to side-step or run around half-a-dozen opponents near his own line rather than hoof the ball to the safety of the touchline. He could lose you a point or two but within a minute of any setback he would strike a beautiful kick between the posts and restore his team's confidence and advantage.

The England selectors could never really make up their mind about Hare. They selected him on 25 occasions at full-back and saw him create goal-kicking records. But what they also did was to impose on him an unwanted record for a full-back. He was dropped from the International side five times. In fact, six others filled the No 15 jersey during that uncertain period. Peter Rossborough, Tony Jorden, Peter Butler, Alistair Hignell, David Caplan and Marcus Rose. Maybe the selectors were nervous of Hare taking chances when the order of the day was not to make a mistake. I have always believed that any full-back can be forgiven the odd error if he is certain to kick the goals. The indisputable fact is that Dusty Hare was responsible for 70% of the points the England team scored during the games he played. Like Bob Hiller before him, I consider Hare was underestimated as a full-back, and taken too much for granted as a goal-kicker. There is no doubt in my mind that had these two been born in Ireland, Scotland or Wales, they would have won many more International caps. That fine coach, Chalkie White, once described Hare as 'an errant genius, more skilful than most and a man with a deep insight into the game'. Rugby needs such heroes for young people to look up to.

He could have played professional rugby for Hull Kingston Rovers but preferred to work his farm and tend his cattle and sheep. He could have opted for first-class cricket with Nottinghamshire, for whom he played during the Gary Sobers era. He chose an amateur game and even donated the royalties from his book to the Newark Rugby Club and Collingham Cricket Club.

The name 'Dusty' was given to him by his father when he was a baby, because of the freckles and little tufts of fluff on an otherwise bald head. Little did Dad know then that the nickname would stick and that that little head would one day be crowned with 25 International caps for England – a record for a full-back. A real cool ball-player.

DUSTY HARE

WATCHING J.P.R., the supreme gladiator on the rugby field – fearless, competitive, adventurous and brave – it was never easy to imagine him as a nine-year-old cherub, a boy soprano who tackled 'Oh for the wings of a Dove', or as a teenager playing first violin in the Glamorgan Youth Orchestra, or at 17 wielding a tennis racket and beating John Lloyd to win Junior Wimbledon in 1966, or singing bass in a Gilbert and Sullivan Opera when he was a medical student at St Mary's Hospital in London. John Peter Rhys Williams is indeed a considerable human being. On the rugby field he became the greatest full-back of his generation and, arguably, of all time. The boy born in Bridgend the day after St David's Day, 1949, has become almost better known world-wide than the patron saint of his country. His deeds are equally well documented.

In 1969 he won the first of his 52 caps at Murrayfield and his entry into International rugby coincided with the introduction of the Australian dispensation law that banned kicking directly to touch outside the '25'. The International Rugby Board must have known J.P.R. was entering the arena for this significant change suited his style perfectly. The full-back would have to run out of trouble rather than kick and J.P.R. revelled in this new adventure. He was still only 20, fresh-faced, wide-eyed and innocent. Wales won that match and then the Triple Crown and Championship. Before he retired in 1981, J.P.R. had been the constant rock of Welsh teams that won six Triple Crowns, three Grand Slams and six Five Nations Championships with one shared. Eleven times he played against England and was never on the losing side, and five of his six International tries were scored against them.

On the field he was instantly recognisable, his fine, straw-coloured hair flying in the wind, long sideburns framing a pale face, white legs with stockings down around his ankles – a warrior committed to battle. From him the spectator came to expect try-saving tackles that would set a seismograph twitching, match-winning tries and dauntless falling and covering. He was never far away from the action.

Tall and powerfully built, he even played flank-forward for Wales on an overseas tour and he was also ideally suited as a prop-forward in the London Welsh seven-a-side team. On Lions tours of New Zealand and South Africa he guaranteed a stout last line of defence and an extra cutting edge to the attack. He switched desperate defence into a try-scoring move in the second Test against New Zealand at Christchurch in 1971. Catching a high kick ahead he ran and ran before linking with Mike Gibson who put Gerald Davies into his stride for a try – and J.P.R. can't remember it for he was suffering from concussion at the time.

Rugby, rather than time, has left its mark on his finely chiselled face. A broken jaw, stitches too numerous to count and one scar left by the boot of a New Zealand prop. During the Bridgend v. All Blacks match J.P.R. was pinned down on the edge of a ruck, head exposed and yards away from the ball. A stud left a hole in his face, he lost a couple of pints of blood before being stitched up and, against all medical advice, returned to the fray.

A Consultant in Orthopaedic Surgery, J.P.R. understands the need for research in Sports Medicine. What a comfort to future J.P.Rs.

J . P . R . WILLIAMS

NOT MANY PLAYERS have scored six penalty goals in an International match but Gavin Hastings achieved that feat in his first International when he scored all of Scotland's points in their 18-17 win over mighty France in 1986. He is the statistician's delight. In four games of the first-ever Rugby World Cup he scored 62 points and, for a couple of hours, he held the world record of 27 points in an International until the Frenchman, Didier Camberabero scored 30 against Zimbabwe in the same competition. There is little doubt that Hastings will easily break the Scottish all-time record of 283 held by the admirable and exciting full-back, Andy Irvine.

Like Irvine, he is raffish – an adventurer who loves nothing better than taking a chance. Although not as fleet of foot as Irvine, he has the vision from the full-back position to join in the threequarter line with devastating effect. With his brother Scott, he has given Scotland an enterprise in attack and an assurance in defence. Perhaps it is in the orthodox full-back chores that he has been most impressive. He is so secure under the high ball and he is big enough to fulfill the crucial task in defence of staying on his feet. Compliments from forwards are rare but one of his team mates said that no one in the pack was troubled when the ball was kicked over their heads for the certainty was that Gavin would be there, eye on the ball and not on the opposition following up, and that he would get the team out of trouble by clearing the ball to the touchline or starting a counter-attack.

When Scotland won the Grand Slam match against England in 1990, his line-kicking was virtually faultless and there was an air of authority about his game that inspired all those around him.

Andrew Gavin Hastings was born in Edinburgh in January 1962 and is one of four brothers, all of whom played for George Watson's College 1st XV and three of whom represented Scottish Schools. Gavin is a loyal and passionate Scot who declined the chance to enhance his International career by joining a top London club like Harlequins or Wasps. Rather he joined London Scottish and eventually as captain guided them back from the Third to the Second Division in the 1989-90 season. His decision spells out the ethic of a man who refuses to be compromised.

When he was a student at George Watson's College in Edinburgh, he was a brilliant all-round sportsman. He excelled at cricket and had the good fortune to be taught the game by the Australian Test player, Kim Hughes. He also finished fourth in the Scottish Boys' Golf Championship, playing off a handicap of six. 'In many ways golf is my first love' says Hastings, 'it is a most pleasurable way of Scottish life to be walking down handsome fairways. But at the end of the day there is nothing in the world to compare with playing rugby for Scotland at Murrayfield. Once you take the field it makes every miserable press-up in training seem so worthwhile.'

Gavin has been an outstanding full-back for Watsonians, Edinburgh, London Scottish, Cambridge University, Scotland, the Barbarians and the Lions in Australia in 1989 when he played in all three Tests and found his peak form at just the right time with five penalty goals in the 19-18 margin that won the third Test and the series. One of Scotland's heroic leaders, Finlay Calder who was the captain on that tour, is generous in his assessment of Gavin Hastings. 'He has such inner belief in himself that he convinces his friends that anything is within his scope. Even when he proves fallible it never, ever shakes his confidence and this is an encouragement to everyone else'.

Off the field, he has a happy-go-lucky demeanour, film star good looks and a sparkle in his green eyes, which are full of mischief. He is not quite as heavily built as his father, Clifford, who was a stalwart forward in the Watsonians rugby team. I played for Cardiff against him during their Christmas tour in the early Fifties, so I know, first hand, where Gavin gets his 'swing of the kilt' from.

GAVIN HASTINGS

DURING A BRITISH LIONS tour in 1977, Andrew Robertson Irvine startled the rugby world by scoring five tries from the full-back position against Colin Meads's King Country-Wanganui. The hardy, immortal New Zealand lock forward could hardly believe his eyes . . . . but that was Andy Irvine, a restless player who was always anxious to be in the thick of things and never happier than when he had the ball in his adhesive hands.

He was sometimes criticised for occasional frailty in the orthodox full-back chores of catch and fall and tackle, but he was not often caught out. More often than not he was secure and he invariably left his opponents grasping and gasping as he weaved his way with marvellous daring through a startled defence. Like one of his famous predecessors, Ken Scotland, he lit up the stage like a flash of forked lightning, flashing brilliantly, thrilling and frightening, and whenever he struck it was devastating.

I remember one of his most memorable performances at Murrayfield in 1980. Andy had missed several kicks at goal and was actually booed by the crowd. With France leading by 14 points to 4 he suddenly erupted and Scotland scored 18 points in 12 minutes and went on to win by 22 points to 14. Andy Irvine's contribution was two tries, two penalty goals and one conversion. What we saw that day was pure genius, a scholarly, swashbuckling performance by a gifted man whose vision was such that he spotted a possibility to attack long before he had the ball himself. He was always on the move, a superb all-round ball player who had the speed of a wing-threequarter – where he played his first senior representative rugby – and could swerve and side-step and punt with great power with either foot. A further attraction was the accuracy and length of his goal-kicking. He was a match winner who made an unforgettable impact on the game.

He once kicked a goal for Heriot's FP at his favourite Goldenacre ground. The ball flew over a wall and broke a window in one of the houses beyond. The ballboys went to retrieve it and were verbally attacked by an elderly lady who came to the door.

'But it was Andy Irvine,' said one of the boys. 'And which one of you is Andy Irvine?' roared the old soul. Such is fame!

Legends may grow old but always fresh in my mind will be a smiling Andy Irvine, sharing a beer and sparkling conversation – his ability to entertain and excite is not restricted to the field of play.

ANDY IRVINE

SERGE BLANCO IS unquestionably a genius at a game which the French play with admirable Gallic improvisation. Since 1980 he has been the throbbing heart of French rugby and he has made the pulse quicken every time he has touched the ball. Whereas the full-back position was always regarded as the last line of defence, Blanco has made it the most exciting position from which to attack. He obviously dislikes restrictions for his first thoughts are of adventure. I am certain that his unpredictability has given the French International coach Jacques Fouroux, many anxious moments. Blanco was actually dropped by Fouroux for the second Test match against Australia in 1989 but not for long could the French rugby supporters be without their favourite virtuoso performer and the diminutive coach had to back down. The cavalier Blanco was a more important ingredient than the matter-of-fact Fouroux. The Basques of Biarritz know and love their rugby and for them Blanco is a god.

The sunshine of the Pyrenees is in his soul and his game reflects it. In the semi-final of the first rugby World Cup against Australia Blanco produced a touch of magic that won the game for France. For me this was the finest game of the whole tournament with both teams playing high quality rugby. With only minutes to the final whistle it looked as if the Final would be played between New Zealand and Australia but everyone had reckoned without Blanco who scored the match winning try in the corner. It was all pace and cunning from a man who believes that the joy of sport is when a player reaches out for the unreachable. He has scored far more tries than any other full-back in the history of the game. 'I don't like to be left out of things on the field'.

His father died when Serge was only two years of age and his mother brought him to Biarritz from Caracas where he was born. In that rugby-crazy town he fell under the influence of Michael Celaya, one of the finest of French rugby players, who saw the natural gifts of the youngster. Ever since, Blanco has shown his loyalty to the club and the people of a town which he loves, and the town loves him. He is quiet, yet witty; private and yet a glamorous symbol for the marketing men. The most radiant, charismatic rugby player in the Northern Hemisphere, however, prefers the simple life at home with his family where, away from the admiring looks of rugby fans, he can sip a glass of fine wine and enjoy the comfort of a cigarette – behind closed doors. 'I don't smoke in public because I would not like to set a bad example to children whom I adore.' The celebrity has moral fibre which he inherited from his mother who has been the biggest influence in his life. His admirable sense of honour and justice is seen in his play on the rugby field. Since he was first capped at the age of 20 he has brought a fresh and warm breeze to the International scene for he believes in friendship and loyalty and fair play. Every expression on his dark-skinned face and in his expressive, dark eyes makes you understand why Serge Blanco is a fine man.

Thirty-five years ago I saw and played against Bob Scott of New Zealand, probably the first attacking full-back the game had produced. He could run and side-step and break a defence when he joined the back line in attack, but I am certain that he was not as fast or elusive as Blanco. Scott could punt the ball with either foot with consistent accuracy and in this he shades the Frenchman. Scott was also a prolific goal-kicker for his country but Blanco does not take that responsibility for France. Considering the fact that rugby is now better than it was in the Fifties and is a yard or two quicker in tempo, I consider Serge Blanco would get my vote as an all-round full-back.

The six-foot Frenchman is a star – whether he likes it or not. During a speech at a Lord's Taverners dinner in London, the former French captain, Jean-Pierre Rives claimed that Blanco was not just a star but the Sun, a person who makes other people warm, and makes them shine. *Vive le Blanco.*

SERGE BLANCO

THE THREEQUARTERS

IT IS AN UNDENIABLE fact that the Welsh are often guilty of overstatement. 'A Welshman's horse is always descended from the one that was ridden by Llewellyn the Great!' But in describing the performance of Gerald Davies for the Lions against Hawke's Bay in 1971 as wonderous, I am guilty of understatement. In a bruising match at Napier he scored four sensational tries and in so doing he bewildered the opposition and astounded the spectators as he flaunted every known skill for beating a man. One try came when he demonstrated blistering speed over 45 yards, another involved two body swerves, the third four side-steps – three off the right foot and one off the left – that left the tacklers clawing thin air while the fourth came from a kick ahead and a long chase, controlling the upredictable bounce of the ball with the skill of a George Best. This was wing-threequarter play of the highest order.

New Zealand is a long, long way from the village of Llansaint in Carmarthenshire where Thomas Gerald Reames Davies was born in February 1945. Like other boys he played football and cricket in the street which was too hard for rugby. Rugby had to wait until his arrival at Queen Elizabeth Grammar School, Carmarthen which had a green, grass pitch. It was there that the coal miner's son picked up a rugby book. It was called *Lions Rampant* written by Vivian Jenkins and it told the story of the adventures of the 1955 Lions in South Africa. He was hooked by the time he came to the last page and decided he wanted to play international rugby. There was no television but the young Davies went to the Regal Cinema at Llanelli where Pathe News showed short clips of the tour matches. The boy in the picture house dreamed dreams and ten years later they became a reality when he ran on to Cardiff Arms Park in the red jersey of Wales to earn his first cap at centre-threequarter against Australia. It was the first of 44 caps and for the next 11 seasons the swerving, side-stepping, dazzling Davies was supreme in a game that favours the adventurer.

Teaching was the profession he chose and he went to Loughborough College. There his rugby flourished under the influence of John Robins, the coach who had been a Lion in New Zealand in 1950. Seven-a-side was a speciality at Loughborough and it was after playing in the Gala Sevens that Gerald was tempted to join the Cardiff Rugby Club which eventually he captained. For a while he taught in the city but he was restless and mindful of the fact that the active days of a sportsman are short. He was keen to get a degree which would advance his progress in education. He won a place at Cambridge and during his vacation he played with London Welsh in the company of J. P. R. Williams, Mervyn Davies, and John Taylor when the club was at its best. Davies was both happy and finely tuned for the forthcoming Lions tour to Australia and New Zealand in 1971. The coach, Carwyn James, gave him special permission to miss the Australian part of the tour so that he could complete his examinations at Cambridge. James knew that Gerald Davies was to be a key figure in his plans to beat the All Blacks. Davies played in all four Tests and the Lions won the series.

Christ's Hospital School, Horsham; The Sports Council for Wales; Director of Harlech Television; rugby writer for *The Times* – the breadth of his experience sustains him and his conversation is never bland. His dark brown, deep-set eyes are sometimes wistful for he is thoughtful and caring. Yet they light up and sparkle when he talks about a try – 'the quickening life of the game that adds to an heroic kind of beauty and creates a legend'. He once explained to me the thing that set the truly great sportsman apart. 'Accepting that you have exceptional talent, you must also have a sliver of ice in your heart.' There was a story going around some years ago that when he was going to bed Gerald Davies could switch off the electric light and be under the sheets before the room went dark. After watching him on the rugby field, I believe that to be true.

GERALD DAVIES

ONE OF JIM RENWICK'S most memorable feats was in a match that his club, Hawick played against their age-long Border rivals, Gala. The 1982 Division One title was at stake. Gala led 10-9 with only seconds to go when Hawick were awarded a penalty. The last kick of the match would decide the Championship. Renwick attempted an easily missable kick from 40 yards as his team mates turned their eyes away. The ball flew straight and true and Jim Renwick did that characteristic ruffling of his receding hairline as the referee whistled no-side.

I only heard tell of that game but I saw, with my own eyes, earlier that season, a wonderful victory for Scotland at Cardiff by 34 points to 18. Wales were beaten at home in the Championship for the first time in 27 matches. It was also the day when Renwick won his 47th cap and his presence in the midfield was awesome. You felt that every member of the Scottish team drew inspiration from his commanding presence, that there was a trace of apprehension in the Welsh side every time he had the ball. He had been in the Scottish sides that had suffered 13 defeats in a row between 1977 and 1980, despite the fact that they had been by far the most attractive International team to watch. It was right that this genuine rugby player was present when the tide turned. He must have loved playing at Cardiff for he is the only Scottish player ever to score a try in three consecutive matches there.

If there were such a thing as a specification for the ideal centre, Renwick would meet 95% of the criteria. He was one of the most difficult of players to mark for he possessed the skills to beat an opponent on the inside or the outside. His jink was such a beautifully timed and executed 'shimmy' that he would leave a defence floundering. Flaring acceleration through the smallest of gaps meant that he made room for those outside him. He was also so strongly built and so immensely solid on his feet, that he was very difficult to tackle. And although he could not knock men back in the tackle like Gavin Hastings, very few escaped the Border man who, in 52 Internationals, gave very little away. And he could win matches with his boot. He scored 67 points in Internationals with eight tries, five penalty goals, four drop goals and four conversions.

He was also a master tactician and his fingerprint was clearly shown on the pattern of every game he played. In one International match the Welsh centres were so positioned that a short pass to a colleague running straight would breach the defence. Renwick spotted this and immediately informed Keith Robertson who took the short pass and made a seering break for a glorious try.

Possessed of a delightful sense of humour, he once made a comment about a try scored from long range by Bruce Hay, not the fleetest of foot in the Scottish back division. 'That is the first time that I have seen the live version and the slow motion replay at one and the same time!' What a pity this talent was only allowed to flourish on one Lions tour, to South Africa in 1980. Jim Renwick, who won his first cap against France a month before his 20th birthday, should have been chosen for three Lions tours. His rich Border accent would have added spice to the expeditions.

When he retired from international rugby he returned to play junior rugby in the town where he was born in February 1952. At Hawick Harlequins he guides and encourages a host of youngsters. A hero, going home, gives a community great pride and hope for the future.

When he was at Hawick High School, Jim became Scottish Schools swimming champion, excelling in the backstroke. This may account for his strong physique. At 38, he has got his golf handicap down to near single figures in just three seasons.

Someone told me, with a smile and in a whisper, that Jim is a golf bandit! I would not know about that. What I do know for certain is that he was one heck of a rugby player.

JIM RENWICK

IN THE AUTUMN of 1988, 22-year-old Will Carling became the youngest captain of England for more than half a century – too young, some said, to span the wide range of responsibilities. Yet within a couple of seasons he raised the drooping spirits of his countrymen by inspiring a new approach that brought a brisk and healthy attacking game which thrilled the spectator and brought results. One Murrayfield nightmare in no way blackened an otherwise bright and glittering winter of 1989-90.

'A captain must keep cool in adversity and refuse to be discouraged by failure.' These words were written 60 years ago by W. W. Wakefield who later became Lord Wakefield of Kendal. He was the most remarkable of rugby men and one of the finest of England captains. Like Wakefield, Will Carling experienced the traditional public-school education of Sedbergh where rugby featured strongly as a game to develop a boy's character, to encourage quick thinking and instinctive reaction … some of the qualities needed in a leader of men.

Schooldays were happy days for the young Carling and he gained 12 'O' and 3 'A' levels in his examinations. He was also bright on the sports field making the Under-15 rugby side when he was only 13. He played full-back and fly-half and was first choice for the 1st XV for three seasons; in a total of five years he was on the losing side only three times. In his final year he captained the English Schools against the Welsh at Cambridge, when the captain of Wales was Robert Jones. The two were to renew the rivalry as men at Twickenham in 1990.

So the seeds of leadership were sown at school and further matured during his time serving in the Royal Regiment of Wales. He had learned from his father – also a soldier and a fine rugby forward who played in the Cardiff pack and appeared in an England Trial – what the Services teach in terms of discipline, method and a built-in responsibility for others. Will eventually left the Army because he was not assured of getting the time off to prepare himself for major matches. He is driven by two ambitions. To prove himself the best centre-threequarter ever to wear an England jersey and to lead his country to a triumphant victory in the 1991 World Cup.

As a student at the University of Durham, he had the good fortune to be advised by a former England and Lions back-row forward, Peter Dixon. The astute Dixon probably changed Carling's life, and when he won an England cap his horizons were broadened further. Psychology was his subject at university and he grew to understand why old-fashioned common sense is the key to so many things. His company, Inspirational Horizons, arranges seminars for businessmen and it focuses on ideas, incentives and leadership in management – priceless qualities in a rugby captain.

He is a fine centre, superbly built for a position that calls for strength in the tackle and speed and guile in attack. He also has that rare quality of being able to change pace when an opening appears. There is also that necessary arrogance of all great players. It was his questioning of the tactics adopted by England in Australia in 1988, when forward domination did not bring results, that eventually turned the fortunes of his country around. For such a young man he has a maturity beyond his years, his shock of black hair and five o'clock shadow help that impression, together with the old-fashioned desire to win with style that for years has been neglected.

Will Carling would like to visit the North Pole and take up flying. Away from the harsh realities of the game he will relax to the sound of Beethoven and Mozart or take a walk in the country, preferably with his sketch book and pencils. Art is a passion. What, I wonder will he make of this caricature?

WILL CARLING

SOMEONE SHOULD HAVE thought of attaching a pedometer to the talented frame of Mike Gibson. The machine would have registered a statistic to baffle the most numerate brain, for the Ulsterman covered more ground than any player I have watched in forty years. Not for one second did he relax, either physically or mentally, and his work-rate was matched by an uncanny aptitude for being in exactly the right place at all times. He could instantly spot changing situations and react with the speed of light. The late Carwyn James, who coached the 1971 Lions in New Zealand, had the highest regard for Mike Gibson. 'Technically the most completely equipped of all the players on the tour. There was nothing he could not do except perhaps believe that he was as good as he was. Others of similar ability would have been insufferable.' Colin Meads, the New Zealand captain, said that Gibson was as near to the perfect rugby player as he had ever seen. Always he seemed to be a few moves ahead of every other man on the field.

He chose Twickenham to announce his intent, first in the University match in 1963 when he made one try and scored another as Cambridge beat Oxford by 19 points to 11. Then on the same field a few months later he won the first of his record 69 caps. He gave a masterful performance as Ireland beat England for the first time at Twickenham for 16 years. He played these matches at fly-half and went on to fill that position 25 times for Ireland. He played four times on the wing and 40 in the centre.

It was in the centre that I thought Mike was most effective and comfortable, quite the best midfield player most of us have seen. Maybe he thought out and analysed the game too efficiently for a fly-half who has to rely so much on instinct. The extra half yard away from the pivot position enabled him to influence the course of a game in a way that only he could. He had such a simple way of doing complicated things.

Playing in the centre he seemed to rediscover the game of his early rugby days when his emphatic style was the quality that set him apart.

Like all eminent artists his timing was immaculate, whether in the tackle or the pass. He made tries and he saved them. His balance was perfection and his scorching speed, through any suggestion of a gap, was a lethal weapon in his armoury.

Mike Gibson was born into a sporting family in December 1942. His mother, Jo, and her sister, represented Northern Ireland at hockey and their father, John Walker, was a soccer international who played for Bury. Grandfather was also hot at billiards; he was Northern Ireland Chess Champion and could complete the *Times* crossword in a quarter of an hour. So the genes were there and Cameron Michael Henderson Gibson simply had to work his socks off to become a star of world rugby in the Seventies. Now he is a successful solicitor in his home town of Belfast, where his work-rate is as punishing as it was on the playing field.

At school he played soccer and was a talented inside forward. His hero was the idol of Newcastle United, Jackie Milburn, rather than the other Jackie – Kyle, the hero of the Irish rugby public in the Fifties. Over the years Mike Gibson became as famous as Kyle and has won the admiration of sportsmen and women around the world, including Gary Player who rates Mike as a golfer.

Before he went up to Cambridge, Mike spent a year at Trinity College Dublin and had his first taste of club rugby with Wanderers under the influence of Ronnie Dawson who captained the 1959 Lions. The Wanderers' 15-man game and reputation for good sportsmanship were to his liking and that is why he was probably at his happiest and very best with the Lions in 1971. That was their style on the tour to New Zealand, where they still rate Gibson as the finest second five-eighth to play there. They are not bad judges.

MIKE GIBSON

THERE WAS A TIME in 1986 when I thought that Rory Underwood would be remembered as an England wing-threequarter who got more caps than passes.

He spent season after dreary International season being ignored by the players inside him and was seldom at the end of a pass leave alone a scoring pass. It was a credit to his metabolism and patience that he didn't suffer frost bite or that his hair did not turn prematurely grey with boredom and frustration. The product of this neglect of a potential matchwinner was that in his first 22 International appearances in an England jersey he crossed the opposition line only four times, and I suspect that was also the total number of times he actually had the ball in his hands.

This was an unrewarding period for England when their approach in attack was inevitably overcomplicated. There was an obsession with conjuring up scissors movements in the middle of the field whenever the backs gained possession. This was made worse when, rather than attempt to create an outside break, the centres ran straight at their opponents and got tackled – the crash ball – in the hope that their forwards would be around quickly enough to create what was called second-phase ball. A sound play as a variation but doomed to fail as a continuous, predictable tactic.

It was Rory Underwood's good fortune that England, under the influence of Geoff Cooke, Roger Uttley and Will Carling, turned to an expansive, flowing game with the result that he has been given the freedom to parade his ability and blistering speed. In 16 International matches he scored 10 tries as England became the most creative team in the Championship, and in January 1990 he broke the record of 18 tries in a career held by Cyril Lowe of Cambridge University and Blackheath who played for England from 1913 to 1924.

In his early International duties Rory seemed to look a little lost in defence and found the positional problem a little difficult to master. This was not because he lacked the courage to tackle and fall but that he had not been made aware of the responsibilities of a wing in defence. He has obviously been made to appreciate the significant differences that set international rugby apart. Advice has paid off and the real Underwood has emerged.

Rory Underwood, who was in the same class as England's fly-half, Rob Andrew, at Barnard Castle School, Durham, was a fine all-round athlete as a boy. He was a classy and swift hurdler, a effective No 4 or 5 batsman and off-spin bowler in the cricket XI and he could swim like a fish. But it was not until John Oates became rugby coach at the school that the young man began to believe in himself, and in his final year he scored 45 tries. Self-confidence paid off and very soon he was selected for England Colts, the Under-24 side, Yorkshire and England 'B' before moving, in 1983, to Leicester where he matured in an atmosphere of adventure and considered rugby for which the Leicester club is renowned. The first of his England caps was not far away.

There is no sight in rugby that compares with a wing-threequarter racing to the try-line and over the years Twickenham has seen some gems. Prince Obolensky's crossfield sprint against the New Zealanders in 1935; Peter Jackson of Coventry – one of the best of all time – side-stepping and swerving and dummying his way to the Australian corner flag in 1958; plus, of course, the five Rory Underwood scored against Fiji in 1989 when he equalled a record by David Lambert of Harlequins which had stood for 82 years.

Built like an old-fashioned Powderhall sprinter, explosive out of the blocks, sturdy around the hips and with the accidental grace of a racehorse on the move, Flying Officer Rory Underwood of the RAF has sprinted his way to the upper tiers of rugby's family and he has done it with superior speed and a ready smile.

RORY UNDERWOOD

AS A TEENAGER, Tony O'Reilly won honours that are only granted to the elect in rugby football. Within months of leaving school at the age of 18, he was selected to represent Leinster, Ireland, the Barbarians and the Lions. He actually celebrated his 19th birthday during the Lions tour to South Africa in 1955 and even then it struck me that he was more mature than the rest of us, for he was both physically and mentally superior to every other rugby player I met in 45 years in the game.

As a young man he enjoyed a wide range of gifts both on and off the field, and he used them wisely and well. He had few peers as a wing-threequarter and since his retirement from rugby in 1970 he has also proved himself in the business world. He is now Chairman of the world-wide Heinz Corporation, the first person outside the Heinz family ever to hold that position. Great men make themselves unforgettable. That is Tony O'Reilly.

Rugby followers in Ireland did not see O'Reilly at his scintillating best for, like many other great players, his talent was neglected because ten-man rugby was the fashion in the home countries during the Fifties. It was on Lions tours to South Africa in 1955 and New Zealand in 1959 that he flourished, scoring a record number of tries in both countries. The comfort for any team is to have someone who is not only fast and strong on the wing but a player who anticipates and scores tries. Tony was all of these things, amazingly quick off the mark for such a big man and so determined when he was given the ball. His acceleration and skill made him a winner. On the South African tour he attracted a fan club for he looked the film star. Tall and superbly framed, his red hair helped to make him a striking figure on the field where he was always exciting to watch. Off the field he was the star entertainer – a brilliant raconteur and wit who could arrest you with gripping tales of famous trials in the Law Courts of Ireland or argue the merits of poets and writers. A considerable man.

Heroes and star performers are there to be knocked down and O'Reilly was accused in Ireland of being reluctant to tackle. On the Lions tour of South Africa I saw him bring down the biggest of the Springboks and fall at their feet without any thought of being hurt. I have a photograph of him carrying three South African players over the line as he scored a try at Ellis Park. Before he played in New Zealand – the country of hard, uncompromising rugby – the people there thought the Irishman with the long legs, the shortest of white shorts and handsome too, would not last on such a demanding tour. They were soon to find out he was tough and constantly exciting to watch, scoring a record 22 tries.

I once asked him how he approached rugby. 'I wait for the game to reveal itself to me before I reveal myself to it. I do exactly the same in my business life.' Tony O'Reilly seldom moves off in haste in the wrong direction. He has the wit and ability to laugh at himself. When the Irish selectors picked him to play at Twickenham, seven years after his last International, he arrived in a chauffeur-driven car and in a pin-striped suit. During the game he had to fall at the feet of the English forwards and got a kick on the back of his head. 'I lay there for a while and then came to through a veil of Celtic unconsciousness and I could just hear a voice shouting "And while you're at it kick his bloody Chauffeur as well".'

Doctor Anthony Joseph Francis Kevin O'Reilly was educated at the famous Dublin school, Belvedere College. The Jesuit priests there set standards and O'Reilly has always maintained them. He is fanatically hard-working and sleeps on average five hours a night as he hops around the world by jet. He is a patriot who cares for Ireland. He is bored by bureaucracy, pomposity and injustice in the world. He is complicated and likeable, does everything on a massive scale but never forgets old friends. All his life he has followed his own star.

TONY O'REILLY

THE HALF-BACKS

IT SIMPLY HAD TO HAPPEN. The very first time Gareth Edwards fished for pike he caught the largest specimen ever seen in Britain – a record weight of 45 lb 12 oz and 'Fish of the Year, 1990'.

So a folk hero of Wales had scored again, another virtuoso winning performance from the greatest all-round rugby player I have ever seen.

The fact that he played 53 consecutive International matches for his country at scrum-half, scoring 20 memorable tries; that during the time he played Wales lost only one match in the Five Nations Championship at Cardiff; that at 20 years and 7 months he was the youngest-ever captain of Wales; that he was the key figure in Triple Crown, Championship and Grand Slam victories; was first-choice on Lions tours of South Africa and New Zealand – each of these is only part of the story of an unbroken colt who turned out to be a priceless thoroughbred.

It was at Pontardawe Technical College that an expert in physical education and a brilliant teacher, Bill Samuel, first saw Gareth Owen Edwards as a 14 year-old who weighed in at 8 stones 5 pounds and stood 5 feet 3 inches on tip-toes. Bill's trained eye saw something that made the heart leap, and he knew that with the right guidance and discipline, Gareth would become a champion. He was right, for young Edwards excelled in the long-jump, the hurdles and the pole-vault, was supreme in athletics and gymnastics, and as a rugby player there were no doubts that he would become one of the greatest.

What the miner's son from the Welsh-speaking village of Gwaen-cae-Gurwen needed was a platform to launch him towards his potential. So, at 17, he went to Millfield Public School in Somerset where he trained alongside a future Olympic competitor, Alan Pascoe, whom he beat in the hurdles to become British Schoolboy Champion.

When he left Millfield the Headmaster, R.J.O. Meyer, wrote, 'I doubt if I shall ever see his like again, for of all the top-class performers in various fields of school activity, he was on his own.'

Gareth Edwards conquered the rugby world in style. The unforgettable tries he scored will live forever. Happily those moments are captured on video tape: the 60-yard try against Scotland at Cardiff in the mud; the dramatic burst to score for the Barbarians against New Zealand at Cardiff; appearing from nowhere to end a thrilling move in Paris . . . there are so many and every one of them was scored at a crucial time for his team.

He had everything, including 360-degree vision. Like the Brazilian footballer, Pele, he was able to see everything going on around him.

He is now Deputy Chairman of Land and Leisure, a subsidiary of Welsh Water. He has fished all the good rivers of Britain, and those of Lapland too.

'If I had to give up rugby or fishing, I'd give up rugby, wouldn't I. I've scored enough tries for Wales, but I haven't caught enough salmon.' That is what he told me on the River Usk one day. He also said that his father claimed that his game went off when the fishing season started because his knees went rusty standing in the water!

A statue of G.O. Edwards stands in a busy shopping precinct in the heart of the capital city of Wales. Even in bronze, you simply have to look up to him.

GARETH EDWARDS

WHEN OLLIE CAMPBELL toured New Zealand with the Lions in 1983, playing superbly in all four Test matches, he had a racehorse named after him. But despite this accolade from the people of a rugby-crazy country, Ollie still has to endure – like all others who have played outside-half for Ireland since the Second World War – comparison with Jack Kyle.

Kyle was the maestro of the late Forties and Fifties. Capped on 46 occasions for his country he was, unquestionably, one the greatest outside-halves who ever played at any time, anywhere, since the game began. But a comparison of players of different eras is not only invidious but unrewarding too. The only sensible judgement is a contemporary one, and I place Ollie Campbell high on the list – very high – for he proved himself a match-winner who always seemed in control. Beautifully balanced and tactically aware, he could make a moderate team look very good. This is an acid test.

In an Ireland-Wales match at Lansdowne Road I watched him score the classic outside-half try. Taking the ball at speed he moved to the blind side of a set scrum 25 metres out. His pace beat the first opponent, a lazy swerve the second and a side-step off the left foot took him over the line. He used every skill in the outside-half canon and that one 10-second flash signalled a truly great player.

He was outstandingly good at school where he played at wing-forward for the Under 9s. By the time he was 10 he had become an outside-half and when he moved to Belvedere College he lit up their rugby. It was from the rich rugby nursery of Old Belvedere that he won his first cap against Australia in 1984, and although he played in the centre several times for Ireland to accommodate Tony Ward – another fine footballer who had a very different style from Campbell – it was in the pivot position that he played in most of his 22 Internationals, and he thought deeply about and planned carefully every one of them.

Before an International he would telephone his great mentor, Father Jimmy Moran, who had coached him at Belvedere College. Father Moran was studying in Chicago during the time Ollie played for Ireland but he would advise and encourage from across the Atlantic. Ollie kept Father Moran in touch by sending a copy of the *Irish Times* every Monday morning. He also took the advice of Dr Ollie Burke who had coached the Leinster Under-19 squad and who watched video recordings and documented the strengths and weakness of the teams Ollie would face at international level.

Seamus Oliver Campbell was a perfectionist as a rugby player and his careful preparation inevitably paid off. But there was much more to him than that. Like John Rutherford of Scotland and Barry John of Wales, he looked so composed and fluent. His running and line-kicking were of a high order and he was a prolific goal-kicker too. He kicked himself into the record books when Ireland won the Triple Crown for the first time since 1949, 46 points in all with 13 penalty goals. In the match against Scotland, which clinched the Triple Crown, he scored all 21 points.

Troublesome injuries caused him to retire in 1987 and the Dublin man who had the ability to make time and room for himself on the rugby field ran and kicked no more. The consolation is that when you meet him for a jar and a chat you still feel the buzz he created in his playing days.

OLLIE CAMPBELL

TWO THOUSAND YEARS before Christ – so *The Story of Wales* by Rhys Davies reveals – a seafaring tribe of short, dark-haired people, non-Aryan, pre-Celtic, settled in Wales. They were short of limb, long-skulled, dark-eyed and volatile of temperament. Phil Bennett of Llanelli, Wales, Barbarians and British Lions is recognisably a descendant.

Somewhere in the roots of his abundant and creative talent is an inherited, ancient Welshness. Not only does he speak the language but he revels in the joys and tribulations of being part of a minority group.

In his game he was singular with an impish genius that made you gasp. There was always a buzz of excitement and expectation when he danced on to the field with those tiny steps. What you knew for certain was that something would happen when he got the ball, for above all he had a sense of adventure. His game was never grim or dull. He had the supreme confidence to augment his daring and an instinct to know when, and what is even more important, when not to break. Judgement is everything and Phil Bennett knew exactly when to turn defence into attack or to surprise the opposition by launching a counter-attack when his team was in trouble.

The most watched try ever, when Gareth Edwards scored in the opening minutes of the Barbarians-New Zealand match at Cardiff in 1972, all started when Phil chased a speculative kick ahead by the All Blacks wing Brian Williams. Facing his own goal-line some 15 metres out he ignored the temptation to kick for the safety of the touch-line. Two huge and spectacular side-steps started the move that broke the New Zealand defence and thrilled millions. This one moment in time was confirmation that Max Boyce's outside-half factory was still going strong and had produced another jewel.

The people of Llanelli unashamedly idolise their rugby heroes. One supporter claimed that he had cured his shingles by touching Phil Bennett's miraculous boot which had kicked three goals against England! The immense Irish lock, Willie John McBride, swears by Phil who was in his Lions team to South Africa in 1974 when they won 21 of the 22 matches. 'Little Benny was the one who made it possible for others to play. He gave me 200 per cent.'

Bennett was himself given the captaincy of the Lions in 1977, but on reflection he wishes he had not accepted the responsibility. With the candour that makes him such a refreshing summariser these days on television, he confesses that he was neither physically nor mentally strong enough to be in charge on such a punishing tour. He did, however, captain Wales eight times and was on the losing side only once. He captained Llanelli to two Cup Final wins in '75 and '76 when they beat Swansea and Aberavon.

When he was born in Felinfoel, near Llanelli, in October 1948, his parents said that he was 'puny and fragile' and that he nearly died because of cervitus gland. 'He will never have the physique to play rugby,' a doctor told Phil's father.

Mr and Mrs Bennett senior did a powerful job, for they raised a rare talent that sparkled as one of the brightest stars of rugby's Milky Way. Greatness, after all, reveals itself in adversity.

PHIL BENNETT

ON THE FACE OF IT, Richard Sharp is the embodiment of what is often regarded as particularly English in rugby football: Montpelier prep school in Paignton; Blundells public school; Royal Marines; Balliol College, Oxford. The truth is that the proud Cornishman is much, much more than the sum of these parts, for not only was he the most beautifully balanced of fly-halves who excited and inspired a whole generation, captain of England in 1963 when they won the Five Nations Championship, but he was also a gentleman whose very presence suggested modesty, honesty and style.

There were 70,000 packed into Twickenham for the Calcutta Cup match in 1963 when R. A. W. Sharp produced one of the greatest individual tries ever seen there. I can see the move clearly as I close my eyes and wonder – after 27 years. From a set-scrum on the 25-yard line (metres had not yet been invented) Sharp took his pass at speed and immediately seemed to be going faster. He threatened a scissors move with Mike Weston but held on to the ball, running around and then through the flat-lying defence before selling an outsize dummy to the Scottish full-back and crossing the line near the posts. England won 10-8 and took the Cup and the title.

Richard spent the first eight years of his life in India where his father, Fred, a mining engineer from the Camborne School of Mines, was working at the time. On 9th September 1938, in Mysore, Mrs Sharp gave birth to Richard Adrian William – a name that would find its way into the Fabled Book of Rugby. He was made a member of Wasps – his father played there – as soon as he was born, but it was to Redruth that he and his elder brother Nigel were taken by Father to see their first rugby match in 1946. The die was surely cast, and the seeds were sown.

It is fair to say that Richard's schooldays were happy. There was an emphasis on sport and he excelled at the pole-vault, the high-jump, rugby and cricket. He was captain of both at Blundells, and in 1957 was wicket-keeper/batsman for Cornwall, playing for his county 14 times. In the same year he was selected for the county rugby side and in his first game managed to play brilliantly before breaking his collar-bone.

At the age of 21 he won the first of his 14 England caps, coming in to the side as last-minute replacement for the talented Bev Risman. He tore the Welsh defence to shreds and was voted Player of the Year as England went on to win the Triple Crown and the Championship.

Like the *Times* newspaper of old, Richard always refers to you by your initials. I was always C.I. Morgan. Today, R.A.W. Sharp lives with his wife and three grown-up children at St Austell where he is Distribution Services Manager for English China Clay. He has been called the 'Redruth Diamond' – an apt label for a rugby player with a cutting edge who sparkled on the field. He was never on a losing side against Wales, but I'll forgive him for, like the diamond, you can't place a true value on Richard Sharp.

RICHARD SHARP

BARRY JOHN shares with Snowdon and Slate, Choirs and Coal, Lloyd George, Dylan Thomas and Richard Burton a fame that reaches far beyond Offa's Dyke. The mention of his name prompts all the ecstasy of a religious revival. In the game of rugby he invented Utopias. He was the first rugby player in the game's history to be instantly recognised – not simply because his boyish features were seen on television but because he created that aura which is in the gift of those who touch greatness in any field. People in shops and offices and in the street who knew nothing about rugby actually knew his name. He was 'King John' to those who played with him and to those who were fortunate enough to watch and wonder.

His supreme confidence made you feel at ease and comfortable, for like the Duke of Wellington he was the master of every situation, unhurried and absolutely in charge, however thick and difficult the battle. Mediocrity was anathema to him for he set high standards for himself. He believed that the game deserved high respect.

When he retired from rugby on 7th May 1972 at the age of 27 and four months, he was generally regarded as one of the finest artists the game has ever produced. 'He was a Church outside-half,' said the Welsh novelist Alun Richards, 'unlike Phil Bennett who was Chapel.' I understand what Richards meant for Phil Bennett was all darting action, snapping here and probing there, unpredictable and excitingly brilliant whereas Barry John was elegant and precise and smooth, almost lazy, never appearing to sweat. He did of course but he didn't show it. Like George Best of Manchester United, he always seemed to have time to do exactly what he wanted to do, and to make everything look so easy. This is a mark of rare talent.

Barry John was a promising soccer player in school at Cefneithin, a tiny village in Carmarthenshire. Gwendraeth Grammar School, which has produced many International players over the years, made him a rugby player, but I am convinced that he could have been tops at any sport he cared to try. Cricket, tennis, snooker all came easily to him for he was an instinctive ball-player. I remember playing snooker with him at Hamilton in New Zealand and cursing him as he potted a red, walked around the table, chatting without watching it go into the pocket, leaving the white ball perfectly placed on the black. His ease and self-belief made me angry and jealous and yet filled me with admiration for an amusing and very nice person.

In New Zealand in 1971 he was the master when the Lions beat the All Blacks in a Test series for the very first time. His goal-kicking was assured, his general play masterful. At Wellington he arrived at the ground with two left boots and yet he contrived to break the goal-kicking record of Gerry Brand!

I have always thought that there should have been a large sign outside every ground where Barry John was due to play: 'Admission £2. If Barry John Plays – £10.'

BARRY JOHN

WENT TO THE dogs with Rob Andrew. It was at Catford Stadium where money was being raised to help a young lad who had suffered a severe spinal injury while playing rugby. Rob had not been selected for the British Lions tour of Australia in the summer of '89 and he was looking forward to the cricket season in the Thames Valley League. But within days he was winging his way to the other side of the world as a replacement for the Irish fly-half, Paul Dean, who had been injured in the opening game of the tour. Rob watched from a seat in the grandstand as the Lions were soundly beaten by the Wallabies in the first Test and then, with Yorkshire grit, played himself into the team that eventually won the series 2 matches to 1.

Chistopher Robert Andrew came of age, took centre-stage and proved his worth. Self-doubt disappeared and he was allowed to play with the freedom all fly-halves must be given. Ian McGeechan, the Lions coach, must take some credit for this for he made Andrew believe that with hard work and application everything is possible. The young man, who six years before had been described by a former England captain as one of the worst players ever to pull on an England jersey has made the doubter eat his words. He has become the most capped English fly-half, leaving great players like Bev Risman, Nim Hall, Tom Brophy, Martin Regan and Richard Sharp way behind.

If Rob Andrew had been born 20 years earlier he would probably have played cricket for England too, for he was a double Blue at Cambridge when he won two University matches at Lord's and three at Twickenham. With the overlapping of seasons and a ludicrous fixture list, these days it is impossible to get to International level in winter and summer sports. Denis Compton, Arthur Milton, M.J.K. Smith, C.B. Fry and Hubert Doggart, who got five Blues at Cambridge and a Test Cap, would have had to opt for one game or another.

At the age of five, Rob wanted to play football like George Best but his love at Barnard Castle School was cricket. 'I dreamed of opening the Yorkshire innings with Geoffrey Boycott, I was sports mad.' On his parents' farm near Richmond, Yorkshire, he had plenty of open spaces right on his doorstep to play games with his brother. Rather than help with the milking he chose to create his own imaginary Headingley, Wembley and Twickenham, little knowing then that one day he would play for Yorkshire 2nd XI, score a first-class century for Cambridge Univeristy at Trent Bridge, and in his first full International for the England rugby team score a record 18 points.

Rob Andrew has experienced the roller-coaster fortunes of International sport. Praised to the heavens one minute and cruelly criticised the next, he has riden it all with great dignity and this tells you why he has made himself first-choice for England and the British Lions. 'I've taken a fair bit of criticism over the years but I've learned to get on with the job and ignore what people say. I used to get worked up into a state before Internationals and was constantly worried about being dropped. I now simply get on with the job.'

John Rutherford and Phil Bennett – two very differnt but equally great fly-halves – are Rob's heroes. I would guess that they, like me, have a high regard for him too.

ROB ANDREW

AS A YOUNGSTER Robert Jones was equally proficient at rugby and cricket and his teachers were convinced that he could have made it to the top with bat and ball if he had not turned to rugby. At Cwmtawe Comprehensive School he was a contemporary of Greg Thomas, the Glamorgan, Northamptonshire and England fast bowler. Facing him one day, Robert was hit on the head by a Thomas 'beamer' but he stood his ground at the wicket and became something of a celebrity in the village of Trebanos where he was born in November 1965. The people of his village have so much more to be proud of these days for their boy, Robert Nicholas Jones has captained his country at rugby.

His sporting record is a remarkable one. He captained the Under 11s at Cardiff Arms Park, led his school to victory at the Roehampton Seven-a-side Tournament and he played 12 times for the Welsh Schools before joining Swansea. He was also capped for the Welsh Schools at cricket – he was a left-hander with all the style of a Viv Richards. The game of rugby can be thankful that Greg Thomas hit him on the head for that one incident probably made up his mind that he would stick to being a scrum-half.

The very best judges of a scrum-half are the outside-halves he has played with. Before he went to Widnes to play rugby league, Jonathan Davies was a big fan of Robert Jones. They played 22 consecutive Internationals for Wales together and Jonathan says that Robert was always half a second faster than anyone else he played with and 'it is amazing what an outside-half can do with this extra time'.

Rob Andrew, the England and Lions fly-half would like to stake a claim to being the number one fan. He considers that his rugby career was given a big boost and a new lease of life when he eventually linked up with Robert in the Test matches in Australia in 1989. 'Until that tour I had never played with anyone like Jones. The speed and length of his pass gave me the room to develop my own game. Another bonus is that he is such an astute kicker and is capable of relieving the situation when the team is under pressure.'

On that Lions tour of Australia, Robert Jones was at his very best and he refused to be overawed by his opposite number, Nick Farr-Jones, who was then regarded as the best scrum-half in the world. During that Test series, Jones came out on equal terms. At 5 feet 7 inches and a little over 11 stones he does not appear to be big enough when the going is tough. But anyone who believes that he can be a push-over gets a shock when the tough, resilient Welshman revels in the cut and thrust. His misfortune has been to captain Wales when its rugby has been at a low ebb and when they were whitewashed in the International Championship in 1990. What is significant is that Robert Jones still contrived to be one of the best players on the field. Greatness is so often revealed in adversity.

He played for Swansea at senior club level when he was still at school. He shares this distinction with one of the greatest scrum-halves ever to play the game, Haydn Tanner. In 1935, schoolboys Tanner and Willie Davies (who later had such a brilliant career with Bradford Northern in the rugby league) were selected to play for Swansea against the 1935 All Blacks captained by Jack Manchester. It is a day that will be talked of for ever – the day Swansea beat New Zealand at St Helens by 11 points to 3 – a day when the great centre Claude Davey scored two tries and two schoolboys became men.

The chirpy, outgoing Jones had an outstanding World Cup in 1987 and was in the Welsh Triple Crown side the following year. He was dropped by Wales after two heavy defeats in New Zealand in 1988. 'A good thing' said Robert with a smile, 'it proves that my father-in-law, Clive Rowlands who is a selector, was not showing favouritism towards me!' The village of Trebanos would have been proud of him for his answer to an awkward question.

ROBERT JONES

GENTLEMAN JOHN – 'Rud' to his friends – always looked immaculate on the field, both in his play and in his appearance. You felt he had bothered to look neat and tidy before he left the dressing-room because he would be on show representing his club or country. John is a stylish man and he could not help displaying an artistry that set him apart. He was the best Scotland stand-off I ever watched or played against.

Poised and emphatic, he gave the impression that he could never pollute the beauty of the game. Rarely did he appear uncomfortable for he had mastered the basic skills which he performed without conscious thought and this left him free to analyse the many possibilities for attacks that could be launched from every part of the field.

Smooth as silk and swift as an arrow, for a stand-off with such long legs he was deceptively quick over the first five yards. He was even faster over the second five, and this was why he was able to beat the close tackler and then glide away into the open spaces. Schoolboys learning the game should study a video of Rutherford in action … and there is plenty available for he played in 42 International matches – a Scottish record. Only one stand-off half won more caps, and that was the immortal Jack Kyle of Ireland with 46.

John's first cap was against Wales in 1979; he scored a try against England in his second International, and until his final game in 1987 against France in Christchurch in the World Cup, when he damaged his knee ligaments, he was first-choice for his country. He scored 64 points in major Internationals for Scotland with seven tries and a record 12 drop-goals. But the record he is most proud of is the world record of 35 cap Internationals that he played with Roy Laidlaw as his partner. I doubt whether this feat will ever be repeated. Laidlaw was energetic, brave and aggressive, and he proved the perfect partner for Rutherford, serving him faithfully and brilliantly. The two had a telepathic understanding seen only in the very best half-back pairings.

John Young Rutherford was born in Selkirk in 1955 and was educated at the High School there. While still a pupil he played for the senior Scottish Schools side in 1972. It is recorded that he was an excellent player but an indifferent punter of the ball. He must have worked hard at this skill for it was his all-round control and pin-point kicking that played such a vital role in Scotland's Grand Slam triumph in 1984.

Even when he was an established international star he stayed loyal to his club, Selkirk, and his fellow Borderers. When he lived for a time in Edinburgh he travelled home three times a week to train and play for his club. He is the epitome of modesty and a self-effacing, fair sportsman. Only once did he receive criticism from the media and that was when he and three other Scottish players accepted an invitation to play in the Bermuda Rugby Festival without obtaining permission to do so from the Scottish Rugby Union. John was badly injured and had to face the prospect of missing a game against Spain at Murrayfield and possibly the World Cup. Some claimed that he had 'let the side down'. But no one could bear a grudge against John Rutherford. He went to the World Cup where he again injured his knee. What irony. His International life, during which he had played so brilliantly for Selkirk, Scotland, the Barbarians and the Lions, was over. John was almost 32.

I will always remember a television commentary by Bill McLaren in 1982 when John scored a try against France at Murrayfield. 'That's his thurrd try in thrree consecutive internationals against France – a real beauty. This fellow Rutherford simply oozes class. They'll be proud of him in Selkirk.' And not simply for that one moment of magic, I'd say.

JOHN RUTHERFORD

THE FORWARDS

IF I CLOSE MY EYES I can see Willie John as clearly as if we were still standing together in the hotel bar on the Sunday morning after the 1971 Lions had beaten New Zealand in the first Test match. He was a commanding figure, clutching a glass of Tullamore Dew in a hand that was the size of a small spade, enjoying the cool comfort of his pipe and looking as thoughtful as an ancient philosopher. 'That was a great win' I offered. 'Forget it, son, that's all in the past. It's the next one that matters now.' And then with a twinkle in his eye he looked down at me. 'Anyway, Morgan, I hate small men.'

Very few rugby men have towered over their contemporaries in the way Willie John McBride did during a phenomenal career than spanned 13 eventful years when he won 63 caps for Ireland and made a record five Lions tours during which he played in 17 Test matches. In South Africa in 1968 he scored the only try his team managed in the Test series. His birthday party there was, as they say, something else. We had wrapped up a gift for him in brown paper. It was a 6 foot 6 inch door – to remind him of the one he had walked straight through a couple of nights before!

Bill is a man's man and is at his most comfortable when in the company of people who share his love of sport and his attitude towards it. No one played with more commitment or harder but he always said, 'Let's have a ding-dong for 80 minutes and a bloody good night after.' The way the Ulsterman played and lived earned him the respect of everyone around him. 'No surrender' was his cry when he captained the Lions to South Africa in 1974. They did not lose a match, beating the Springboks 4-nil in the Test series … a suitable climax to the life of a rugby servant who travelled the rugby world and conquered it.

He was born and reared on a 50-acre farm where he shared the chores with his sister and brothers. Working the land made him physically and mentally tough and equipped him for the fierce battles that lay ahead. So the young McBride from Moneyglass, near Toomebridge, County Antrim grew into a colossus who made his presence felt in every facet of the game, as player, coach and manager of the Lions team.

In 1969 we were making a film together and had left the bank in Coleraine where he was working at the time, and spent an hour recording an interview on the river bank. When we arrived back at the bank it had been raided. 'And where the hell were you, Bill?' he was asked. 'Doing the important thing, talking rugby with the little man.' People always felt as safe as houses when Willie John was around. If he had been there, there would not have been a raid!

He has a fine tenor voice and with a little coaxing will treat an audience to a song or two. My vivid memory is of him singing in the Ballymena Club – he's the President now …

> *Will ye go Lassie go,*
> *And we'll all go together,*
> *To pluck wild mountain Thyme*
> *All around the blooming Heather,*
> *Will ye go Lassie go.*

There is always a song in Willie John's heart.

WILLIE JOHN McBRIDE

DURING THE LIONS tour of South Africa in 1980, Fran Cotton had to spend some time in hospital. One of his visitors was the eminent surgeon, Dr Christian Barnard who, jokingly, offered him a new heart. It was Peter Wheeler, the outstanding England and Lions hooker who retorted, 'You could carry out a search in every country in the world and you would never find a heart big enough to replace Fran's'!

Everyone who played with Cotton will swear that he was the greatest of prop forwards because apart from every other quality he possessed, he could play tight-head or loose-head prop with equal facility at the highest level. In a rugby age of specialisation we may never see his like again. Everyone who played against him in the front row of the scrummage will admit that he was physically and mentally tough. They will also add that the Englishman, who had great strength and a fanatical dedication to fitness, was a good bloke to be with because he had a deep feeling for the game and a respect for those who played it hard. He was a merciless foe but he played fair.

He knew all about hard forward-play for he was born in Wigan in the heart of Rugby League country and as a boy watched and wondered at the brilliance of Billy Boston who set the game alight whenever he ran with the ball. Fran's father, David and his brother Dave, or 'Big D' played for Warrington and so there was rugby in the blood. At Newton Le Willows Grammar School and at Loughborough Colleges the young Cotton played the Union game and worked hard to perfect the skills. His reward was 31 England caps and 7 appearances for the Lions in Test matches.

He first played for the England Under-23 side against Fiji and made his full International debut against Scotland in March 1971 – the day Scotland won at Twickenham for the first time since 1938. He was one of the reserves for the Lions tour of '71 and later toured Japan and the Far East with England but he did not play International rugby again until 1973 when he featured in all the Championship matches before going to New Zealand with England and playing in the front row when the All Blacks were beaten 16-10 in Auckland. He went back to New Zealand with the 1977 Lions and was first choice for all four Test matches and it was a battle-hardened Cotton that returned home. Injury after two Internationals and then a troublesome achilles tendon problem robbed England of a giant in the pack. He then dislocated a shoulder but recovered in time to play his heroic part in the North's historic victory over the touring All Blacks at Otley. In 1980 he was a totally reliable team mate in the Grand Slam team led by his close friend, Bill Beaumont.

I have often wondered if Wales would have beaten England in 1981 if Fran Cotton had not been forced to leave the field with a leg injury. He had a burning desire to be in an England team that was victorious at Cardiff Arms Park. England, denied the presence of the phenomenally competitive giant, lost the game in injury time.

Sadly, Fran Cotton did not play International rugby again. He took advice from his doctor. Continual knocks and kicks to the bottom of his left leg had caused the natural drainage channels in that part of his body to become blocked. Consequently any bacteria that penetrated through broken skin in that region would become lodged there and cause infection. There was no way he could keep playing the game, hoping he would not cut or graze his leg. Whenever I visit Jeff Butterfield's Rugby Club in London I see Fran Cotton – a massive man with a powerful frame topped with a noble head and lantern jaw. He is covered from head to toe in mud but you are still aware of his honest, open eyes. He dominates the dining room. It is, of course a 10-foot blow-up of of a photograph – and yet you get the feeling that in his company you can still 'warm your hands'.

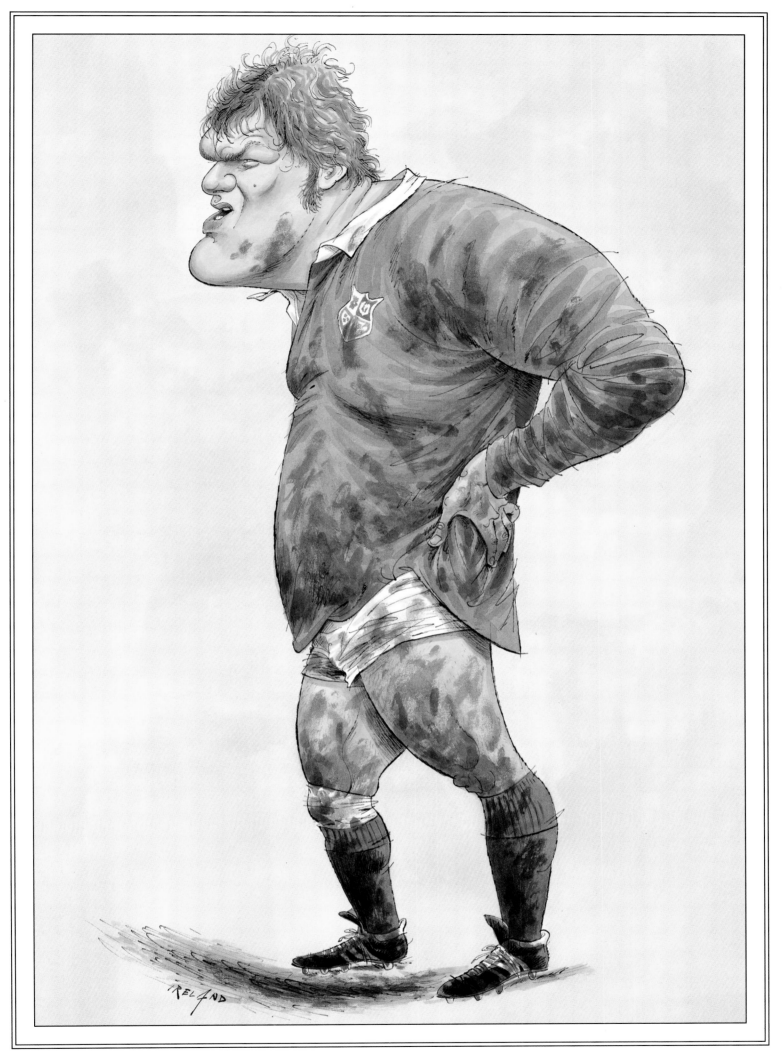

FRAN COTTON

THIRTY MINUTES INTO the semi-final of the Welsh Cup match between Swansea and Pontypool at Cardiff Arms Park in 1976, Mervyn Davies collapsed after suffering an intercranial haemorrhage. 'There followed a fortnight's gap in my consciousness, no discomfort, no pain, no dreadful trauma – just a lost 14 days. That's a long time out of anyone's life, especially when you're 29, ostensibly in your prime and used to a non-stop round of positive living in vigorous, active company.'

He is now fully recovered and as active as when I first saw him play for London Welsh in 1969. At the time he was a raw 23 year-old, keen as mustard and so obviously relishing being part of the running game that was the club's style in those days. He stood out, coal-black hair that seemed to frame his white face and the white sweatband he wore to reduce the prospect of a cauliflower ear. Although he had a strong upper torso, I thought his thighs a little slender for a forward, but it didn't seem to affect his strength in the scrum, his jumping in the line-out or his speed around the field. In the years that followed he became the inspiration in Welsh and British Lions teams.

I got to know him well during the Lions tour of New Zealand in 1971 when you could plot his performances on the field with a straight line on a piece of graph paper. Never once did he fall below the high standards he set for himself and I rate him alongside Brian Lochore of New Zealand, Hennie Muller of South Africa and Des O'Brien of Ireland as one of the all-time greats in the No. 8 position.

He played for Wales 38 times – nine as captain, when his team lost only one game in winning a Grand Slam and a Championship twice. His pedigree was right for his father played for Wales in Victory Internationals after the Second World War. I saw a couple of those matches at Swansea, where Mervyn was born in December 1946. At school he played soccer and it was not until his teens that he appeared in regional and Welsh Schoolboy trials. He played only one game for Swansea before a teaching post attracted him to London, and there at Old Deer Park his rugby life was enriched under the influence of John Dawes whose curriculum encouraged adventure and skill, creativity, fitness and, above all, enjoyment. This philosophy marked the '71 Lions Tour when Mervyn played alongside some of the finest players of all time. Carwyn James, the coach, was a deep, intellectual thinker about the game and went about his business quietly. Mervyn shares that reserve for seldom will you hear him pontificate. But when he does speak you listen for there is good sense and wisdom.

It was only six weeks after his first game for London Welsh that he was picked to play for Wales against Scotland. The selectors took a chance but time has proved that they were so right to go for the Quiet Man.

MERVYN DAVIES

CIARAN FITZGERALD is Ireland's most successful captain since the days of Karl Mullen whose team included the celebrated Jack Kyle, Noel Henderson and George Norton in the backs and the indestructable back row of Jimmy McCarthy, Des O'Brient and Bill McKay. Mullen's team won the Triple Crown in 1949 and it was not until Fitzgerald led the Irish in 1982 that the mythical trophy went back across the Irish Sea. Ciaran Fitzgerald needed all the inner determination which guided him to the top because he had been dropped after holding his place for the whole season following his first cap against Australia in 1979. He was ignored and then brought back as captain in 1982. Ireland won the Triple Crown – a prize that had eluded them for 33 years.

He was the first to admit that his rugby talent was, in some areas, limited but it was plain to see that when the Irish team was under pressure in that fiery cauldron known as the Five Nations Championship, he was able to inspire his men to new heights. He is assured of a place in Irish rugby history for he led from the front when he captained his country to a second Triple Crown. In an awards ceremony at Trinity College Dublin in the early part of 1990, he was chosen as hooker in the Irish team of the decade, a selection of the best players of the Eighties.

To be a successful captain is a rare gift and for Ireland Ciaran filled the role which came naturally to him for he had the cool discipline he acquired as an Army officer. His youthful face and urchin fringe hair cut belied the strength of character of the man from Galway who believed that anybody chosen to play in the green jersey was fortunate.

As captain of Ireland he had the knack of getting things done. He accepted nothing short of maximum effort. Like the French, the Irish have so much talent as individuals and the need is for someone to pull it all together and to have a cool head when things go wrong. He might not have been the greatest hooker every to play for his country but his energy in the broken play was an example. Another example he set was in physical fitness and he was as lively at the end of a game as he was at the kick-off.

The pinnacle of his rugby career was being named captain of the 1983 Lions to New Zealand. He was the seventh Irishman to lead the Lions since Sammy Walker was in charge in South Africa in 1938. The 1950 Lions to Australia and New Zealand were captained by the Irish Hooker Karl Mullen. Robin Thompson led the Lions to South Africa in 1955 and it was Ronnie Dawson, like Ciaran Fitzgerald a hooker, who took the talented Lions to Australia and New Zealand in 1959. Tom Kiernan, Ireland's full-back captained the Lions in South Africa in 1968 and it was of course Willie John McBride's Lions who went through South Africa unbeaten in 1974.

So it was that Ciaran Fitzgerald followed this long line of Irishmen but his was not to be a vintage side. He himself had trouble throwing in to the line-out and came under fire, mainly from Scotland's touring media because they thought their hooker, Colin Deans should play in the Test matches. During this onslaught no account was taken of poor team selection or the undoubted superiority of the All Blacks. 'That tour to New Zealand proved the most bitter period of my life, but I have since put it down to experience and consider that I am a better man for it' said Fitzgerald philosophically.

It is the rather shy Galway smile of this son of Connacht that strikes you when you meet him. His genuine pride in his country and his love of rugby will make him a most valuable coach to Ireland's International team.

CIARAN FITZGERALD

FORGETTING ANCIENT RIVALRIES, modern battles in the Borders are conducted between those rugby clubs which have, for so many years, provided the backbone of Scotland's International team. It was 90 years ago that a Hawick player, W. E. Kyle, became one of the first 'working men' to win a cap. Since then a constant flow of talent has been nurtured at Mansfield Park. Colin Thomas Deans is one of the finest.

Scotland's captain in the first-ever World Cup was born in Hawick in 1955 into a rugby-playing family and followed his father, Peter, into the hooking berth of the Hawick team. Indeed, when he wrote his autobiography he chose as a title, *You'll be a hooker then* because of an incident he remembered at Trinity Primary School when he was a tiny boy. He tells the story of how his games teacher, Bill McLaren, on asking his name then enquired if he was Peter Deans's son. When the lad answered that he was, McLaren who had played for Hawick with Peter, said to the youngster 'Right, you'll be a hooker then'. By the time he retired, Colin Deans had become the most capped hooker in the world.

He first played rugby at the Trinity School and then the High School before joining the semi-junior Hawick Wanderers and graduating to the junior Hawick Trades side. The graduation process is a real strength as young players are not pushed too early in their lives. It is also an inspiration when you mix with rugby folk who have a pride in a club's past. Everyone who lives around Hawick seems to know everything there is to know about rugby, and in this atmosphere great players are made. Colin himself has helped to form the Hawick Albion Club which aims to provide fixtures for lads in the Under-16 group.

At 5 feet 10 inches, Colin Deans is no giant but by application and sound technique he turned himself into one of the fastest hookers the game has ever seen – not only as a striker of the ball in the scrummages but in 'haring about the paddock' as they say in New Zealand. The rugby people in that country, who know about forward play, had enormous regard for Deans who performed in a typical All Black fashion. The Lions tour there in 1983 was his only tour with the Lions and there is no doubt that he was frustrated by the presence of the other hooker, Ciaran Fitzgerald, who was also the captain and followed precedent by playing in all four Test matches. Although many people said that Deans was the better hooker and all-round player, he didn't seem to let the situation gnaw too deeply. It does say a lot for the Scot that he always put the team first and proved himself an outstanding tourist.

Touring overseas gives you a good insight into management and behaviour. Deans must have learned much and when he was elected captain of Scotland he put everything he knew into the task. No leader has been more capable of leading from the front and ensuring the forwards' concentration for the whole game; inspiring them with his own brand of Border fervour; never allowing them to wilt under pressure. When you add to these qualities a perception and a caring for everyone in the team then you know you have a leader. He captained Scotland 13 times and, having led his country in the World Cup, was given the honour of captaining the British Lions team against the Rest of the World at Cardiff during the International Board Centenary in 1986.

Congenial, gregarious and warm with a tremendous sense of fun – that is what men who have played with him say. He is a frequent visitor to Wilton Lodge Park on a Saturday morning to see his oldest son, Roddy, playing as an 11-year-old for the local Primary School. Another case of 'You'll be a hooker then'? I hope so.

COLIN DEANS

THE SPORTING CREDENTIALS of Andy Ripley, Corinthian and non-conformist, are above suspicion. There is not an ounce of greed or ego in his massive frame. Offhand, I cannot think of a more caring sportsman whose presence has enriched the lives of so many people. 'Ripley,' said the celebrated French breakaway forward, Jean-Pierre Rives, 'is a fantastic man, a great person and a great rugby player. Unlike so many others, he never made the mistake of taking himself too seriously.' Maybe this is why he appeared to enjoy his rugby with the Barbarians and with Rosslyn Park, the club he joined in 1971 and played for with everything he had for 18 years.

He represented England on 24 occasions, 12 of them in a formidable backrow with Tony Neary and Peter Dixon. I remember when he was selected for his first cap in 1973 and a headline in one of the daily papers read, 'Ripley – the first Hippie to play for England'. What England actually got was a fine athlete. He was a member of Polytechnic Harriers and ran the 400 metres hurdles in the AAA Championships in 1978. His ball skills and adventure brought life into a game which at that time lacked artistry and finesse among the forwards.

Andrew George Ripley was born in Liverpool on the first day of December 1947. At the age of seven he went to live in Bristol where soccer was his first love. He played centre-half in the team at Greenway Comprehensive School and was a keen supporter of Bristol City. It was not until he went to read Social Studies at the University of East Anglia that his interest in rugby was fired by the former Cardiff, Wales and British Lions wing-threequarter Haydn Morris, who saw his athletic potential and proceeded to nurture it.

Young Ripley was an adventurer, and at the end of his second year at University he went to the United States of America on the 'Hippie Tour' and followed this with a trip to Afghanistan. He took nothing for granted and wanted to find out for himself. He's a more interesting companion for all this. In his company you are never bored and you can bet on a laugh or two. Andy is a most entertaining after-dinner speaker.

In the early Eighties, Andy Ripley took part in television's 'Superstars' with enormous success. He won the British and European Crown and came third in the World event. Typically, he gave all his winnings to charity. He did the same thing with the proceeds from the first edition of his trilogy of books called *Ripley's Rugby Rubbish*. This time it was the National Society for the Prevention of Cruelty to Children that benefited. But it is his giving of time, that most precious of all gifts, that makes him so special. I remember him busily organising a lunch for a Rosslyn Park supporter who needed a special car to carry himself and his wheelchair. The special lunch raised £7000.

He is a chartered accountant; he has worked in the City as General Manager for the Bank of Kuwait and he now works for a company called Espree Leisure in London. He lives with his family near Lingfield racecourse and my bet is that he is a very happy man.

ANDY RIPLEY

JOHN JEFFREY gained some notoriety for his part in damaging the Calcutta Cup in association with the England No. 8 forward, Dean Richards, following the Scotland-England match at Murrayfield in 1988. But it is not for this one moment of high jinks after an International match that I will think of. him, rather as a relentless, marauding, breakaway forward who had the skill to destroy and create. He is the blond version of W.I.D. Elliot who played for Edinburgh Academicals and won 29 caps for Scotland between 1947 and 1954. Elliot was the most difficult flank-forward I played against for not only was he a hard man with considerable speed but he had something more than the expected anticipation. He had intuition – a sixth sense. Very early in my first International at Murrayfield he picked me up under his right arm as if I were one of the sheep on his farm, squeezed the life out of me and then dropped me to the ground. 'Now you know what playing international rugby is all about, son'.

Like Elliot, John Jeffrey is a son of the soil – a farmer who works 1800 Border acres of the family farm at Kersknowe near Kelso and is kept fit chasing 400 head of cattle and sheep. One look at him and you begin to understand why he is physically and mentally tougher, stronger and fitter than so many of his opponents. His hard, open-air life ensures that there is not one ounce of fat on his granite frame. He always looks finely tuned and ready for action. He has already scored nine tries in major Internationals for Scotland, more than any other forward in the history of the game.

He was fortunate to be educated at St Mary's prep school in Melrose and at Merchiston Castle School in Edinburgh, two famous rugby nurseries. It was inevitable that he would play for Kelso, the team he led to the Division One championship in the 1988-89 season.

When he was first capped, against Australia in 1984, Jeffrey carried on something of a Kelso tradition in the rearing of big, raw-boned loose forwards, for he was the fifth in a line that was started in the Twenties by the much-feared and famous Jimmy Graham, follwed by Ken Smith, Charlie Stewart and Eric Paxton. It is no coincidence that four of them have been farmers, while Paxton was a rugged agricultural engineer.

For some years now, John Jeffrey has been known as 'The White Shark', not for the reason implied but because he does not take kindly to the sun. On a tour of Bermuda with the Penguins, his lilywhite frame was observed coming out of the sea and the nickname was promptly applied. He is a fearsome predator all right, but he is also equipped in the skills that make him the complete player, a player's player.

I will also gamble that he will be the topic of a rugby quiz question of the future: 'Which Scottish International forward also played for Wales?' The answer: John Jeffrey, who replaced Aled Williams in the Welsh team in the semi-final of the Hong Kong seven-a-side tournament in April 1990.

JOHN JEFFREY

GRAHAM PRICE was born in Moasca, a hundred miles from Cairo, Egypt on 24th November 1951. His father was a sergeant-major in the Royal Army Ordnance Corps. By the time he was 25 Graham, along with Bobby Windsor and Charlie Faulkner, had been immortalised by the rugby Bard of Wales, Max Boyce, who documented the deeds of a trio that packed down together in the Welsh scrum in 19 full Internationals. 'We may go up and we may go down, but we NEVER go back' – that was their motto and suddenly everyone at Cardiff Arms Park was singing in unison 'The Ballad of the Pontypool Front Row'.

> There's a programme on the telly,
> I see it when I can
> The story of an astronaut
> The first bionic man.
> He cost 6 million dollars
> That's a lot of bread I know
> But Wigan offered more than that
> For the Pontypool front row.

This was the first time a club front row had represented Wales. A further honour came when they were chosen *en bloc* for the Lions team to New Zealand in 1977.

Graham Price has the distinction of having played more Test matches for the Lions than any other prop-forward, and his 12 Test appearances are more than any other Welshman in any position. He is the most capped Welsh forward with 41 International games. In February 1983 he passed the 38-match record held by Mervyn Davies. How ironic that after that Wales-England match at Cardiff the selectors' axe fell. But not for long could his country play without the Prince of Props and he was recalled to play against Ireland and France and then be selected for his third Lions tour to New Zealand where he played in all the Tests.

Price was more than a solid frame and fine scrummager. He placed an emphasis on strength and speed and he proved himself the perfect aide to the expert line-out jumpers. The front of the line was rock solid with no gaps. His technique and selflessness were not overlooked by his fellow forwards. For a sizeable man, committed to the expected graft of a prop, he was surprisingly mobile and athletic. In his first International against France in 1975 he hacked forward and chased the ball for 75 yards to score a thrilling try near the end of the game. He silenced the Parisian crowd.

At the age of 11, Graham went to West Mon Grammar School – a fine rugby nursery – and he won five caps for the Welsh Schools Under-19 side in 1968-69. The following year he won the Welsh Schools Discus and Shot titles and he could easily have developed into an international athlete. Rugby would have missed him and the game would have been deprived of a world-class talent.

He knew, at 18, that he wanted to be an engineer and he is now a civil engineer in Cwmbran. He also knew that he wanted to play rugby and was fortunate to come under the influence of Ray Prosser, one of the finest tight forwards to wear a Welsh and Lions jersey and for me the most amusing and kindly of human beings. Ray coached Pontypool and Price. Pontypool became Welsh club champions and Price a victor.

He retired from International rugby but continued for his club for five seasons and at the end had played 552 games for Pontypool. But that was not the end for he was coaxed out of retirement in 1989 to face again the touring New Zealanders. For the twelfth time in his career, the quiet and reserved prop took on the All Blacks. They knew he was there.

He was sincere, conscientious, unruffled – even when a punch from Steve Finnane broke his jaw in 1978 when Wales were touring Australia. Above all, perhaps, he was reliable – both on and off the field.

GRAHAM PRICE

THE SIGHT OF MOSS KEANE on the rugby field suggested indestructability. The sight of him walking towards you after a game dictated that you were in for a long night with plenty to drink, lots of laughter and fun and if you were lucky only an hour in your bed. Moss had worked out that if you spent the statutory eight hours in the comfort of your bed, by the time you reached 60 you would have slept for 20 years. This he regarded as a nonsense – a complete waste of time. Life was for living, or better still, for living it up. There were never enough hours in the day to enjoy the company of friends.

His accent was not easy to understand but it was worth perservering for he was one of the funniest rugby men I have ever known. He was also a truly great forward – the most Irish of forwards – who never shirked the fire on the field; he was fearless and he was never uncertain of what was expected of him. His giant frame filled the Irish jersey 51 times and never once did he give less than one hundred per cent. 'He's one hullava man,' said a famous All Black forward, and the New Zealanders know a hard man when they meet one.

Moss is built like a telephone box with sharp edges and he has a face that is strong and craggy with wicked eyes that seem gentle and understanding. He's all gristle and bone, but above all he has a big heart. He was educated at St Brendan's College in Killarney, a town of unsurpassed beauty, where he first made a name for himself as a Gaelic footballer, representing Kerry at junior level and then playing for the University of Cork when they won the County Championship and the Sigerson Cup. In addition he played for the University in the All Ireland Senior Football Final and for Kerry in the All Ireland Junior Football Final. He also played rugby at University, was soon in the senior side and progressed smoothly into the Munster provincial side, making his début in 1972-73 when they won the Championship. One year later, at the age of 25, he gained his first cap against France in Paris. He toured with the Lions in New Zealand in '77 and a year later was in the Munster team which beat the All Blacks 12-nil in a famous victory at Thomond Park – the only Irish team ever to have beaten the New Zealanders.

Moss Keane has filled every minute of his rugby life with an enthusiasm and a happiness that is infectious. When he retired in 1984, a little colour went out of Irish rugby ... the big man left an enormous void.

Standing with Moss's father one day, Willie John McBride asked him, 'How did a little fellow like you standing 5 feet 1 inch produce a giant like that?' 'Oh,' came the answer, 'he's a Kerry freak.' A Kerry rugby legend too.

MOSS KEANE

THERE IS A remarkable photograph of Ian McLauchlan hanging an 18½-stone New Zealand prop-forward up to dry in a scrummage. This is just one exmple of the remarkable scrummaging feats of a man who, at the age of 21 in his first Scottish Trial, was considered by the 'experts' to be far too small for an International forward. He was only 5 feet 9 inches tall and weighed a touch over 13 stones. What the doubters had not considered was the fact that sound technique could overcome brawn. 'Mighty Mouse' eventually played in 43 International matches for his country and he distinguished himself with some outstanding performances at home and overseas. Some of his opponents claim that he almost re-wrote the textbook of front-row play during his ten years of International competition – hard lessons from the dark recesses.

When Scotland played England twice on consecutive Saturdays in 1971, the front-row tactics had been somewhat unceremonious and after the first match at Twickenham it is reported that one of the England forwards said, plaintively, 'We don't play like that down here.' Whereupon McLauchlan was said to have replied, 'Well, sonny boy, you've got a week to find out just how to do it!'

Ian reminds me in many ways of a Scottish prop-forward I toured with in 1955. Hughie McLeod of Hawick was also small by today's standards but he had remarkable strength and sound technique and only once in his career was he ever troubled by an opposing prop. That was in 1961 when he played for South of Scotland against South Africa and faced the hard Boland farmer Piet du Toit. Hughie McLeod was, like Ian McLauchlan, forthright and uncompromising, and good company off the field. McLauchlan was a combative forward who understood his obligations to his team and his country. Nineteen times he captained Scotland in official Internationals and 12 of the matches ended in victory. His passionate and fiery team talks did the trick.

He learned his trade from a senior lecturer at Jordanhill College called Bill Dickinson who became 'adviser to the Scottish captain' – the term 'National Coach' was frowned on in those days, it smacked of professionalism! Dickinson had made a detailed study of the art of scrummaging, and by following his theories McLauchlan soon became renowned for his strength, craft and technique, time and again getting the better of bigger and heavier opponents.

When he scored a try for the Lions in the first Test match in Dunedin in 1971, I was 65 feet up on a scaffolding built outside the ground over the pavement and some 50 yards from the near touch-line. 'Mighty Mouse' chose the far touch-line to score, surrounded by at least a dozen players in black and in red. Through a pair of borrowed binoculars I recognised his gnome-like shape burrowing over the New Zealand line and then, at the full extension of the lens, his face – grinning from ear to ear and showing a fine set of teeth. When I spoke to him after the game about his try he told me that it was nothing new because he had scored 15 tries from the prop-forward position for his club, Jordanhill, before he had even played for Scotland.

When he ended his career he had played 19 seasons with Jordanhill. He was 37 years old and still smiling, having made an indelible mark upon the forward game.

IAN McLAUCHLAN

VALEUR! THAT IS THE word that springs immediately to mind when I think of Jean-Pierre Rives. The indelible memory is of Rives storming around the rugby fields of the world with wondrous *élan*. For a man who appeared small compared with other International back-row forwards, he certainly made his presence felt, creating havoc amongst opposition backs and yet always in the thick of the forward battles. His handsome face still bears the marks of combat, scars over his eyebrows and teeth replaced after a French club match that took its toll. It was not too often that you saw Rives in a match without blood somewhere on his face for he ventured into the territory where rugby hurts. He thought nothing of this for the injuries were the result, not of foul play by another player, but 'abrasions that come in a game where you have to take risks – and what would rugby be without risks'.

His was a refreshing attitude. He bore no grudges and went about his business of hounding and tackling and creating with gusto. He was always scrupulously fair – a disciplined adventurer who was intelligent and remorselessly fit. He cut a fine figure on the field and the French players bowed to him as their captain and leader. During its history, French rugby has been blessed with so many remarkably gifted players but very few captains who have had the ability to harness this talent and create stability without destroying the natural flair. Lucien Mias of Mazamet was one who did this in the mid-Fifties and ten years later, Michel Crauste of Lourdes was a shining example on tour in South Africa in 1964. My memory of Crauste's leadership was in the match against Wales in 1965 when he inspired one of the most striking examples of total rugby. Jean-Pierre Rives is very much like Michel Crauste for he too is a prophet of rugby *à la française*. Both have been invested with the Legion D'Honneur, Crauste by General de Gaulle and Rives by President Mitterand. The French are unashamed of their sporting heroes.

In France, Rives receives the adulation of a film or pop star for he represents to the young that untouchable figure who is chivalrous and warrior-like and whose deeds set him apart. The young ladies adore him for his good looks, trendy clothes and manliness. He could be the action man who beats all the obstacles to secretly deliver a box of Black Magic. The boys want to imitate him for, like the swashbuckling d'Artagnan of the Three Musketeers, Rives belongs to the dreams of what they would love to be.

In Africa, where he was brought up, he played tennis and it was not until he was in his early teens that he took up rugby when his family returned to Toulouse, the town where he was born. 'It was my father who pointed me to rugby because he thought me too drowsy for tennis.' Having dipped his toe as a wing, centre and scrum-half, he took to the flank of the scrum and won a French schoolboy cap, a French Universities place and recognition in the French B side before his first full cap at Twickenham in 1975 when England were beaten by 27 points to 20. London is a favourite town of his for it was at Twickenham that he led the French team to a Grand Slam in 1981. He rates Paris and London his top cities. Wherever he goes he attracts attention. I would guess that he would have enjoyed long coffee-drinking hours in smokey Paris cafés with painters and writers, musicians – anyone who wanted a chat. He loves music, poetry, books and beautiful women. The dilettante image he creates hides a deep-thinking young man who at heart is an idealist. He will tell you, in good English, though he sometimes pretends he has difficulty, that he plays rugby, not as a profession but for the joy it gives him. He dislikes dirty play for it is frustrating and unfair. He fits perfectly the Barbarian Football Club's attitude to the game of rugby and he treasures his membership of that club. He has won every honour the game can offer. 'The toughest thing about success', wrote the songwriter Irving Berlin, 'is that you've got to keep on being a success.' Jean-Pierre Rives, with the flowing yellow hair and magnetic personality, can't fail.

JEAN-PIERRE RIVES

WHEN I WAS 18, on my first tour with the Cardiff Rugby Club, I was lucky enough to share a room with Cliff Davies who played in the front row with such distinction for Wales, the Barbarians and the British Lions. I have had a soft spot for prop-forwards ever since for they inevitably exude that delicious difference which comes from living cheek by jowl with the opposition buried in the darkness of the scrum. Theirs is a freemasonry which is impossible to understand or penetrate.

I remember writing an article about prop-forward play in the *Sunday Times* in 1959 and the following Saturday attending a Welsh Trial at Newport. The first person I saw was Ray Prosser of Pontypool. 'What's all that rubbish you wrote in that thick paper last week, Cliffie? You know nothing about us in the pack. You was one of them primadonnas in the backs!' Until now I have never repeated the error but take this chance – not in any technical way – but by a respectful nod in the direction of Gareth Chilcott of Bath, England and the British Lions. He has found himself at the centre of controversy a few times when he has been sent off the field but for me the shortcomings in one direction have been more than made up in others for he has been a kind and fatherly figure to youngsters and to the disabled in particular. He cares for others and is a loyal team man, dedicated to training and fitness and the welfare of his fellow man whoever he may be. I pardon him his odd sin on the field when a short fuse has let him down. He is, after all, my kind of man – amusing to be with on tour, with a sense of fun and the ridiculous.

The irony is that had there been suitable work for his father, David, in Ogmore Vale in Mid Glamorgan, Gareth Chilcott would have played for Wales. But his mother and father had to move to Bristol and it was there on the 20th November 1956 that Gareth James Chilcott was born. When he was at Ashton Park Comprehensive School his first love was football and he followed Bristol City all over the country until he was advised by his games master, Mr Ridgeway, that he was keeping the wrong company and that he should channel his aggression into rugby. He joined Old Redcliffians and played hooker for them, then was invited to join the Bath club in 1975. He was in the first team within a few weeks and has been first-choice ever since. On 5th May 1990 he played in the Pilkington Cup Final for Bath against Gloucester. It was his sixth final at Twickenham – a record he enjoys sharing with Richard Hill who has played so effectively for England at scrum-half and who is the best and fastest passer of the ball from that position I have ever seen.

The same could not be said for Gareth but, after all, that is not his job. He's the grafter who sets things up for others which is what he does in his everyday life too.

I asked him in a radio interview how he would describe his shape. 'Like an eighteen-stone pear,' he said with a chuckle. Well, he has attracted various knicknames such as 'Coochie' and 'Oddjob' (after the James Bond character), but I like to think of him as a priority candidate for any event I would choose to attend.

GARETH CHILCOTT

LIKE ALL THE SUPERIOR flank-forwards who have played International rugby, Fergus Slattery tended to 'cross on the amber light'. He strained every nerve to arrive at his target at precisely the same moment as the ball. He seemed to love flirting with danger and no opposing half-back ever felt comfortable or confident when the most-capped flanker in the world was around. Sixty-one times he wore the green jersey of Ireland and he played four Test matches for the Lions.

Some flank-forwards are good workers in the scrummage and close play and others quick and conspicuous about the field. Slattery was no seagull for he was equally at home in the hardness of a dour forward struggle as he was in broken play when his deadly trackling, speed and adhesive hands were a priority. Few men I have seen could match him and he seldom fell below the high standards he set himself during an International career that spanned 14 seasons.

At 21 he played his first game for Ireland against South Africa and he was quick to adjust to the pace and ferocity of the game which was very different from his club rugby with Blackrock College and University College, Dublin. I watched his first match for Ireland and clearly remember his pale face with tight lips and impassive expression as he stalked his prey one moment and then joined in the rough exchanges with the giant Springbok forwards the next. This match was the start of a phenomenal career at the highest level for Slattery who saw full-back Tom Kiernan kick a last-minute penalty to give the Irish an 8-8 draw at Lansdowne Road.

He also experienced the joy of the Irish when the team won the Championship in 1974 for the first time in 23 years. Then came two Triple Crown successes when Ciaran Fitzgerald led the team. Slattery, with all the know-how from hard, competitive years was an inspiration and gave the team the confidence to play well above itself. He was an inspiration. Off the field, and in the dressing-room, he was the wit.

If he had played in the 1920s he would have relished the company of the legendary figure, Dr Jammie Clinch, for their attitude to playing games would have coincided and they would have shared that distinctive Dublin sense of humour. There is a story told about Jammie of an afternoon when he was sitting on the rail outside Trinity College where he was a medical student and an American lady emerged from a tour of the College and spoke to him. 'It's a big place, I've been three hours going through it,' she said. Jammie replied, 'Ma'am, I have been here seven years and I am not through it yet.'

Fergus, like Jammie Clinch, was popular with his fellows, for he made a contribution to the game and to good conversation. He was a top tourist because he lifted the spirit of others with his sense of fun and the ridiculous. Because of work commitments he was not available for Lion tours to New Zealand in 1977 and '83 or to South Africa in 1980, otherwise he could have come near to the remarkable record of 17 Test match appearances of his fellow Irishman, Willie John McBride.

He did tour New Zealand in 1971 and went on the all-conquering Lions tour to South Africa in 1974 when they won 21 of the 22 matches played. On that tour he trained very hard for he believed that the more you trained the more enjoyment you would get from playing. He was fast and persistent, trained with the backs rather than the forwards, and over 50 yards was faster than most. The only match that prevented the team from being invincible was the final Test against the Springboks at Johannesburg which ended in a 14-14 draw. Fergus Slattery, and everyone else who saw the game, thought he had scored the winning try but the referee was not satisfied that he had grounded the ball in the proper fashion.

I have no idea what Fergus said about the referee but knowing him I would guess that it was in a soft Dublin accent – and not very loud!

FERGUS SLATTERY

LONG BEFORE I SAW him play in his first International match for Wales in 1967 – the same day that Gareth Edwards won the first of his 53 caps – I was a fan of Dai Morris. Watching him play for Neath you marvelled at his work rate and wondered how he was able to combine the chore of adding weight to the scrummage with his skills at the tail of the line-out, his deadly tackling and his lightning speed around the field.

What we were looking at was an exceptional rugby talent who had the tenacity of a corgi, snapping at the heels of his pack and faithfully doing all the things that were asked of him. He was a scrupulously clean player who would never resort to dubious behaviour. His honesty and selflessness suggested everything that is good and wholesome in the game.

As a man he possesses old fashioned gallantry and he understands the debt we all owe to society. He is not the sort of individual who would 'cop out' for he relishes a challenge. Upright is the word I would choose to describe a man who's fundamental obligation is to other people.

'Dai the Shadow' – what an apt nickname, for on the field he appeared to be attached to his half-backs by a piece of elastic and was always close at hand to support or protect. Whenever there was a break by one of the backs, Dai was at the elbow, eager to get involved. Gareth Edwards and Barry John claim that with Dai around you were encouraged to 'have a go' because he gave you the confidence to try to beat the opposition in the certain knowledge that if you failed, Dai would clear up. In his 34 Internationals he scored six tries but there were countless others that would never have been scored without him.

The job description for back-row forwards in the Nineties will call for giants at 6 feet 4 inches weighing 15 stones. The irony is that Dai would not have qualified for he was a mere 6 feet and a shade over 12 stones in weight. But he was all sinew and bone and there was not a pick of spare flesh on him. The secret of a back-row forward is to make every ounce and inch count and few in the history of the game have done this better than Morris.

The South African flanker, Piet Greyling and New Zealand's captain, Graham Mourie were very similar and like the Welshman, they never seemed to be more than five or six yards away from the ball wherever the action was on the field. Another thing all three had in common was the ability to make a smothering tackle, gain possession and immediately start a counter-attack. Greyling and Mourie were perpetual motion and superfit. Dai never trained for physical fitness because he was never out of condition. His hard-working hours at the blacksmith's anvil at the Tower Colliery kept him fit and as hard as nails.

The closing of the pits could have meant that Dai would be condemned to industry's waste but he spends his time caring for a hundred sheep and the horses, which are his great love. As a schoolboy he had an interest in ponies but his pride now is breeding racehorses at his home in Rhigos. The Neath coach, Brian Thomas, had played rugby at Cambridge with Ian Balding, the famous racehourse trainer, and Brian decided to give Dai a treat, and to get him some professional advice. At that time Balding had Mill Reef in his yard at Kingsclere and when Dai saw the horse he was speechless. 'Dai was dribbling with excitement.'

He has a 14-year-old mare in foal and she has produced some fine offspring. If she yields another beauty they should name it 'Shadow'. If it is anything like Dai it should be a winner. One thing is certain, it will be a favourite.

DAI MORRIS

DAVID SOLE IS AN HONOURS GRADUATE of Exeter University, a one-time schoolmaster and now a grain buyer for United Distillers Cereals Ltd. He also happens to be the captain of Scotland's rugby team and many fine judges forecast that he will develop into the most influential figure in the game in years to come. He has that gift of leadership. In rugby football there are plenty of lieutenants but precious few generals. Sole has come up the hard way and is battle-hardened, full of valour and tactically and strategically aware. General Sole for certain.

It has been reported that one of his favourite books is Mark McCormack's *What they don't teach you at the Harvard Business School*. I wonder if he got the idea from its pages of walking rather than running his team on to the field before the Grand Slam match against England in March 1990. No rugby manual would have prompted that master-stroke of psychology which produced a moment that Murrayfield had never experienced in its long history. To the measured steps the enormous crowd sang 'Flower of Scotland' and the full-throated sound made the hairs stand on the back of your neck and quickened the beat of what you hoped was your heart. It was a surprise and a shock tactic that appeared to reduce members of a really brilliant England team to mere mortals. Round one to Sole.

The 5 feet 11 inch, loose-head prop forward, weighing 16 stones 4 pounds, has come a long way since he was given a hard time by Ireland's Des Fitzgerald in a 'B' International in 1983. He has now become a prop of great strength and craft and can hold his own against the most disruptive of opponents. He leads his team in a quiet undemonstrative way and during the Lions tour of Australia in 1989, when he played in all three Tests, he led the Lions against New South Wales 'B' and the Anzacs. The Scottish selectors were so impressed that they appointed him captain against Fiji in preference to Finlay Calder who had captained the Lions so wonderfully well. When Sole was asked to captain the Home Unions XV against Europe at Twickenham it was proof that he could command the respect of men from all Nations. His authority could cross all boundaries.

From Exeter University, Sole joined the Bath club and played his first game against Bristol in 1984. There he got a taste of the demands at the very top level of the game and a thorough grounding in the basic arts of prop-forward play. He was in the Bath team in the 1987 John Player Cup Final. He also had a season with Toronto Scottish when he was in Canada on a teaching exchange there. Now he is in his third season with Edinburgh Academicals. He gained the first of his 25 caps to date as one of six new caps in a Scottish team that beat France 18-17 at Murrayfield in 1986 and has now become an outstanding modern-type prop-forward. His play reflects scrummaging strength, adhesive hands that make him a secure sweeper at the line-out and a body position in driving play that fits the New Zealand requirement for 'spines in line'. The former Scottish Schools prop is superbly fit and has an instinctive feel for support play.

There was a time when prop forwards used to plead that they couldn't be expected to shove *and* think. The tradition of loose-head props leading Scotland has disproved that. Ian McLauchlan was captain for a record 19 times and he was followed by Jim Aitken who led his country to their first Grand Slam in 59 years. David Michael Barclay Sole is the rightful heir. He was captain of cricket and rugby at Glenalmond School and it must have been a fine school for it taught a young man about courtesy and courage, discipline and decisiveness – qualities that set some men apart.

DAVID SOLE

LIKE SOLOMON and his wisdom, Ray McLoughlin was light years ahead of his time. He dismissed the old adage that rugby forwards should not be expected to think as well as shove. For him there was more to playing international rugby than honest grafting in the pack and the line-out.

When he was elected captain of Ireland in the mid-Sixties he apparently infuriated some of his team mates because he insisted on hours of concentration during the build-up to a big game. The haphazard approach was not to his liking. A couple of Munster players were reported to have been upset by 'all this thinking'. That was 25 years ago. Today the McLoughlin method is accepted as essential in the highly competitive world of rugby.

Unfortunately, in the Sixties, the Irish selectors seemed to have been influenced by the doubters and McLoughlin was removed from the captaincy. It cost him the leadership of the Lions to New Zealand in 1966 but he was selected as one of the prop forwards. On that unsuccessful tour he became convinced that the forwards playing in Ireland, England, Scotland and Wales would never match the All Blacks unless a great deal of thought was given to the technicalities of scrummaging, rucking and line-out work. Without first analysing the objectives, improvement was impossible.

As a player, Ray McLoughlin admitted to having limited natural flair but he used his sharp mathematical mind to teach himself how to turn and drive and use his strength and weight to maximum effect. He was one of the first forwards in the home countries to use weights to build upper-body strength. He played 40 times for his country. He and Willie John McBride won their first and last caps in the same matches. They also share a dedication to the game which they served when rugby was moving into a period of change. McLoughlin reformed the organisation of the Irish team with new practice sessions and better communication between players.

No one should underestimate his contribution to the celebrated success of the Lions in New Zealand in 1971. A few days before the Lions set off Carwyn James was deeply disturbed by the prospect that his master plan to beat the All Blacks would be wrecked if he could not ensure that Ray would make the trip.

McLoughlin was concerned whether he could afford the three months needed as he was about to launch himself into a business career – which has since become an enormous success story. Eventually James, with his charm, persuaded the talented Irishman to make rugby his top priority for one more tour. James was aware that the Lions had backs like Mike Gibson, David Duckham, Gareth Edwards, Barry John, John Bevan and so many others who would, given the ball, destroy any New Zealand side. To do this the forwards had to gain parity in the bitter battles. The presence of Ray McLoughlin proved the key, for he helped to develop a pack of forwards that not only outscrummaged the All Blacks but adopted a line-out technique to counter the methods the New Zealanders had used for years to overwhelm the opposition. Sadly McLoughlin broke a thumb in the unsavoury battle at Canterbury a week before the first Test. But so deeply was the McLoughlin method ingrained in the other props, Sean Lynch and Ian McLauchlan that they stepped in and helped the Lions to win the series 2-1.

He left that tour early because of his injury and everyone was sad to see him go. The company director who gained a science degree at University College, Dublin was a good travelling companion. His dry sense of humour never failed to amuse. He once confessed that he would never have broken his thumb if he had hit Alex Wyllie properly when the boots started to fly in that Canterbury game. There was a twinkle in his eye.

RAY McLOUGHLIN

ON THE BBC's SPORTS QUIZ, 'A Question of Sport', Bill Beaumont leaps out of the screen and rivets you. He makes you feel secure. His eyes tell you all there is to know about the big man with an almost walrus moustache and you wonder at the breadth of his knowledge, his wit and generosity and, above all, his adroit captaincy. You instantly understand why, and indeed how, he gave England's rugby team the confident leadership to win the Grand Slam in 1980 for the first time since 1957 when another Lancastrian, Eric Evans of Sale, led his troops from the front.

What is difficult to comprehend is the sight of him playing at fly-half or full-back. But that is exactly how he started at Ellesmere College at the age of 14 when he came under the influence of a former England player, Ian Beer, who is now Headmaster at Harrow. Bill's first game for the Fylde club was in the 6th team at full-back, but he soon became a flanker and then a prop. He made his first appearance for the 1st team against Waterloo in November 1970 and within two seasons was a regular in Lancashire's county team.

Bill's rugby life has been eventful to say the least. In 1975 he won the first of his 34 caps when he replaced Roger Uttley against Ireland. (During a train journey to London for a training session Roger had injured his back when he bent over to pick up a piece of apple pie!) In Australia with England that year, Bill had to move to prop forward in one of the Internationals when Mike Burton was sent off! During his half-time team talk in the Australia match at Twickenham in 1982, Bill failed to get the complete attention of his men. He was the only one of the 15 that missed a daring 30-metre sprint by the well-proportioned streaker, Erica Roe. It was the advice of a consultant neuro-surgeon and not 'anno domini' that ended his colourful career. Playing for Lancashire in the County Championship final against North Midlands, he had to leave the field with impaired vision after receiving a kick on the head. Bill took the doctors' advice and called it a day.

William Blackledge Beaumont took easily to leadership, and those who fell under his command followed without questioning. So, Lancashire won the County Championship and England the Triple Crown, the Championship and the Grand Slam. Twenty-one times he captained his country and his team were victorious 11 times. He played seven Test matches for the Lions and in 1980 he became the first Englishman for 50 years to captain a Lions team.

At his prep school he opened the batting for the 1st XI and later played circket for Chorley in the Northern League when one of his team-mates was Paul Mariner who became an England International footballer. Bill also supported Blackburn Rovers football team, and sport, at the time, was the centre of his life. His father played rugby for his Cambridge College and for Fylde and his uncle, Joe Blackledge, was captain of the Lancashire Cricket Club for a time in the early Sixties. Bill's pedigree was fine.

It may well be that in 20 years' time Bill, like Henry Cooper before him, will still be an instantly recognisable personality. Already people who know him through 'A Question of Sport' may not be aware of his stature as a sportsman, but he will continue to be recognised by people able to discern a genuine article.

BILL BEAUMONT

A REFEREE,
TWO COACHES AND
A COMMENTATOR

ONE OF THE ENTERTAINING stories that Clive Norling regales his audience with at rugby club dinners refers to the existence of a headstone in a cemetery in Swansea. It stands over the grave of a man named Thomas William Griffith James. The inscription reads: 'Here lies an honest man and a referee!' Then with a twinkle in his eye Clive adds: 'So that proves that we bury two in the same grave in Wales.' The man who is regarded by most as the best rugby referee in the world understands that you should not take yourself too seriously and that being too earnest and stiff has a way of antagonising the listener. He applies the same rule when he uses the whistle.

Rugby, for the Neath man, is about enjoyment and satisfaction and laughter and delight and something worth being part of. Any action that breaks his code gets little sympathy. Having been a player and a qualified coach he seems to understand what the vast majority of rugby players need from a referee. Thus he gives every game he controls a chance to move freely with as few stoppages as possible. It is no coincidence that the five Oxford-Cambridge matches he has been invited to regulate have turned out to be so attractive to watch and, according to the players, marvellous to play in.

Clive Norling went to Neath Grammar School and played as a second-row forward on Saturday mornings and then refereed a game in the afternoon. He was only 17 when he took charge of his first match and this gave him a taste for refereeing, particularly when he was forced to stop playing when he injured his back in a match against Millfield School. He first became a member of the Neath and District Referees' Society and then during the five years he spent on a Business Studies Course at Portsmouth Polytechnic he joined the Hampshire Society.

He was only 23 years of age when he took charge of the match between the Metropolitan Police and Bristol and sent off one of the Met Police players. During his career so far 49 players have left the field after misconduct. He does not take these decisions lightly but firmly believes that one idiot should not be allowed to spoil the enjoyment of others. Happily there are today other International referees who are prepared to make this judgement and they need the support of rugby administrators. I recall when the Welsh referee Ivor David, also of Neath, sent off the Australian forward Colin Windon at Llanelli in 1948. It was six years before he was given an International match by the Welsh Rugby Union. Times, I hope, have changed, for as rugby gets more competitive the referees need to know exactly where they stand. Mind you, administrators take some unbelievable decisions as they did at the first World Cup in Australasia in 1987 when Clive Norling, known to be the best referee attending, was sent home before the final matches.

He cuts an impressive figure on the field: a big man, which adds to his authority; a natty dresser with trim shorts and a modern hair style. What he does is to spell out his authority with a quiet word here and a rough tongue there. Discipline with understanding is his way and most players respond and enjoy the freedom of expression that this brings. He had the courage to issue marching orders to Jean-Pierre Garuet in front of a packed house in Paris in the Ireland game in 1984. Garuet was the first Frenchman to be sent off in an International.

He treats rugby players in exactly the same way as his students at his college in Swansea. 'At the end of the day it comes down to management. It is better to have a knowledge of the game than of the Laws. If you don't it's a recipe for confusion.' He makes it sound so easy.

CLIVE NORLING

TEN MINUTES AFTER, Scotland's Grand Slam victory over England on St Patrick's Day 1990, Ian McGeechan was asked about Scotland's prospects for their Summer Tour of New Zealand. With a tiny, arcane smile he responded, 'Well, the trouble is that after this, the All Blacks might begin to take us seriously.' The Head of Games and the Humanities at Fir Tree Middle School, Leeds, is not simply the finest of coaches but a realist. His vision is not blinkered and nobody could accuse him of complacency.

He is steelier than most, refusing to allow the British Lions in Australia to fret after being overwhelmed by 30 points to 12 in the first Test match in 1989. He absorbed the Press criticism and treated the many doubters in rugby's administration with firmness but great charm. He was a quick learner and, with an exceptional eye for detail, turned defeat into victory in the following two Internationals. In doing so he earned the respect and admiration of Englishmen, Irishmen, Welshmen and his fellow Scots, not to mention the rugby men of Australia, for his team swept through their country with only one defeat in 12 matches.

Ian McGeechan has taken coaching to a new plane and we lesser mortals would do well to have the grace and wit and humility to copy. Progress is about watching and listening and considering, then making up your own mind – the successful McGeechan formula.

He won the first of his 32 caps against New Zealand at Murrayfield in 1972. Playing at stand-off half, he dropped a fine goal. He had educated feet and a particularly stong left foot which he often used to telling effect. A wonderful versatile midfield player with safe hands; he was for his size – 5 feet 9 inches and weighing a little over 11 stones – a courageous and copybook tackler. These qualities made him a key figure in Lions teams in South Africa and New Zealand in 1974 and 1977.

Ian could well have played cricket for England. As a 16-year-old, left-arm medium-pace bowler he attracted the attention of the Yorkshire County Cricket Club who invited him to the nets under the eye of the famous duo, Bill Bowes and Arthur Mitchell. Ian once bowled at Geoffrey Boycott in the nets, and was good enough to take wickets for Hunslett Nelson in the tough Yorkshire League. He played cricket for Yorkshire Schools but, eventually, rugby won his patronage. Ian Robert McGeechan has served the game well.

Although born in Leeds, on 30th October 1946, he is a passionate Scot. His father, Bob, was a medical orderly in the Argyle and Sutherland Highlanders and was severely burned when his ship was hit by German dive-bombers during the evacuation of Crete. He was taken to the special burns unit in Leeds and it was there that he met Ian's mother, Hilda. There was never any doubt, though, that the young McGeechan would wear the blue jersey of Scotland. Few have done so with such style and pride.

He has also given so many rugby players an unshakable faith in their own abilities as, with meticulous care, he has studied and tested all the options in a game which demands so much at International level. What he has also done is to pay tribute to the men who have shared his work and success: Jim Telfer, a former Lions coach who helped to engineer Scotland's Grand Slam in 1990, and Roger Uttley of England, who stood shoulder to shoulder with him and the Lions in Australia. McGeechan is the quiet man with a stiff stubborn strap to his backbone. His work-rate is prodigious. The only time he can really relax is at home with his lovely wife, Judy, and their two children. He deserves that.

IAN McGEECHAN

NOBODY WHO SPENDS time in the company of Roger Uttley can possibly walk away without a feeling of reassurance. His eyes are full of knowledge and understanding and he always lends a willing ear. Perhaps we take for granted an oracular rugby man like Roger, for he is unassuming and doesn't wear his talents and achievements on his sleeve. For a man who has contributed so much to the game he is reluctant to take praise and you somehow know that he has a genuine pride in the success of others. During his playing days he was an honest forward who accepted and understood the graft that was his duty and as a coach he is committed to excellence and positive rugby.

'A good coach makes the players coach themselves in an atmosphere of mutual respect' says Uttley philosophically, 'I have learned this from bitter experience.' He belongs to a new breed of enlightened rugby coaches. He does not attempt to impress his players with complex tactical ideas, dazzle them with affected rhetoric, outline plans that are unlikely to work during the heat of a game. He simply concentrates on making his players feel good and grown up, putting the onus on them so that they display the necessary qualities on the field. He understands that however well you set up an international coaching system, it is of little use unless your players have both talent and the right attitude.

In partnership with Geoff Cooke, he has lifted the spirit of England's International team and with the Scotsman, Ian McGeechan, on the Lions tour to Australia in 1989, he formed an outstanding coaching duo. While the deep-thinking McGeechan concentrated on the tactical plan for success, Uttley prepared the forwards for the tough battles ahead. He did it with ruthless discipline and plenty of good humour.

The hard, craggy-faced Uttley was an exceptionally versatile player. In his 23 International matches for England he packed down in the second row of the scrum 11 times, he played seven times at No 8 and five times as a flanker. Watching him play over many years, I think he was happiest when playing in the back row. In 1974 in South Africa, he played all four Test matches on that record-breaking tour and scored a try in the final Test which ended in a 13-13 draw. There he combined with Fergus Slattery and Mervyn Davies in a back row that is regarded as the best ever to represent the Lions.

Away from his life with the Lions, there can be no question about the finest back-row performance for him. It was a bleak autumn day in 1979 in Ottley, Yorkshire when New Zealand suffered their biggest defeat on British soil. In the North back row that day were Peter Dixon, Tony Neary and Roger Uttley. On that memorable afternoon, they taught Graham Mourie's All Blacks a lesson in how to play winning rugby. The irony is that this formidable trio played together in only one International for England. Uttley did however captain England in all the Championship matches in 1976-77 when he was also in Gosforth's winning side in the John Player Cup at Twickenham. His last four Internationals were in the Grand Slam team of 1980.

Roger Miles Uttley, born in Blackpool, educated at the local grammar school and Northumberland College is now Director of Physical Education at Harrow School. I was once invited by the Headmaster, Ian Beer who also played rugby for England, to speak to the senior boys in the lovely chapel there. I told tales of rugby and the privilege of taking part in sport; of fair play and courage; of the feeling of well-being that comes with physical fitness; of understanding other people's problems and how to spend your life not only agreeably but well. Over a cup of tea one of the senior boys approached me. 'Excuse me, Sir, but Mr Uttley has already told us that'.

Ah well, beaten to the post by Uttley again!

ROGER UTTLEY

IN 1966, LONG BEFORE the fungoid growth of corporate hospitality had taken hold at sporting events. Bill McLaren invited David Coleman and me to lunch at Murrayfield. 'It'll be out of the boot of my eight-year-old banger, son, but the eats will be great 'cos Bette will see to that.'

When the boot of the car was opened there, as promised, was a feast prepared by Bill's lovely wife. What we were not prepared for was the sight of 14 rugby balls and 16 golf clubs – 11 of them, I recall, were No. 5 irons. It turned out that Bill had begged, borrowed and probably stolen this loot from his friends so that the boys at the primary schools where he taught Physical Education could have the equipment necessary for them to experience the joy of playing games. 'I believe in the old-fashioned theory that rugby, in particular, shapes a youngster's character. It teaches them discipline – that delicate balance between freedom and accountability.'

The experience of that lunch spelt out for me all the things I wanted to know about a man who was so obviously created by the topography and myths of the Borders of Scotland.

William Pollock McLaren was born in Hawick on 16th October 1923 and he has lived there ever since. 'The only way they are going to get me out of here, son, is in a box!' It was at Trinity Primary School that the young McLaren learned his five-times table and he returned there to teach Physical Education years later after passing through the High School and Woolmanhill College in Aberdeen. One of the boys he coached was the then 11-year-old Colin Deans who was to become Scotland's World Cup captain and a British Lions hooker in New Zealand in 1983. Bill left teaching for nine years when he worked on the *Hawick Express,* covering Council meetings, Court proceedings and local news. In 1959 he returned to teaching and was in charge of Physical Education at four primary schools in Hawick. One of his star pupils was the legendary Jim Renwick who played 52 Internationals for Scotland. Others were Alister Campbell and Tony Stanger who scored the vital Grand Slam try against England at Murrayfield in 1990.

From the time he was a toddler, Bill dreamed dreams of wearing the blue jersey of Scotland himself. But fate struck a cruel blow, for after war service in Italy with the 5th Medium Regiment, Royal Artillery, he contracted pulmonary tuberculosis. His rugby days were over. The rampaging flank-forward of Hawick was denied the cap he would have undoubtedly won after playing a trial in 1947. McLaren, a big man in every way, took it on the chin and faced two years in the East Fortune Hospital in East Lothian. A miracle cure – attributed at the time to a new drug called Streptomycin – gave Bill the strength to overcome his illness. Scotland may have lost the presence of a fine forward but television gained a giant. For almost 40 years, his has been the voice of rugby ... instantly recognised in the far-flung corners of the world and loved by everyone. He goes everywhere without compromising his rich Border accent. He's no pseudo television personality for his feet are firmly rooted in his native soil; he cherishes the comfort of a lovely family, Bette his wife, his twin daughters and their children. Only once did I really sense a touch of over-emotion in a McLaren commentary and that was when his son-in-law, Alan Lawson, scored a couple of remarkable tries for Scotland. He's allowed that. Why is he the best? Bill McLaren loves broadcasting, but he loves the game far, far, more.

BILL McLAREN

ACKNOWLEDGEMENT

The Publishers would like
to thank Colin Elsey of Colorsport
for his help in providing photographic references
to assist John Ireland in the
development of his caricatures.